SPURRED TO SUCCESS

SPURRED TO SUCCESS

GLENN HODDLE with Harry Harris

Queen Anne Press
Futura

A Queen Anne Press/Futura Book

First published in Great Britain in 1987 by
Queen Anne Press, a division of
Macdonald & Co (Publishers) Ltd
3rd Floor
Greater London House
Hampstead Road
London
NW1 7QX

A member of Maxwell Pergamon Publishing Corporation plc
This edition published in Great Britain in 1988 by
Queen Anne Press/Futura

Jacket photograph: Colorsport

ISBN 0-7088-40086

Reproduced, printed and bound in Great Britain by
Hazell Watson & Viney Limited
Member of BPCC plc
Aylesbury Bucks

To Mum, Dad, Anne and Carl

ACKNOWLEDGEMENTS

There are many people who have helped me both in the course of my career and in writing this book. Although it would be impossible to mention all their names here, I would like to thank the following people whose assistance and advice have been invaluable: first of all Alf Pearce, who spotted me on a football pitch and set the ball rolling; my former Spurs team-mate Johnny Gorman, now Gillingham's youth team coach, who has always been a good and honest friend; Monte Fresco, for the beautiful photograph of my two daughters that appears in this book, and my wife Anne for persuading me to include my own baby picture!

Last but by no means least, I would like to thank Andy Porter for compiling my career statistics, Harry Harris for helping me to put my thoughts into words – although his spelling is even worse than mine! – and my editor, Caroline North, who has tried to correct it.

Contents

Introduction

He has been described as the 'White Pele'; he has Diego Maradona among his admirers; yet, despite his rare gift for inspirational skills, he has remained English soccer's greatest enigma for more than a decade. Glenn Hoddle provokes almost violent debate among fans, managers and football journalists alike. Some say he is a genius – others condemn him as gutless. Managers at the highest level are divided on the question of whether they would choose Hoddle for their team.

The 'Hoddle argument' is more fundamental than a simple assessment of an individual performer – it highlights the deep and often disturbing morality of the English game. Are we too dependent on workers and runners? Should we develop the more complex artists? Can we afford to 'carry' the play-maker who does not bear the responsibility of defensive duty?

Those questions have haunted Hoddle for his entire career, ever since the time he scored a wonder-goal by inventing an unorthodox side-foot drive from outside the box to score on his England debut against Bulgaria at Wembley at the age of 22. He should have forged onwards to have won 70 caps by the 1986 World Cup finals in Mexico. Instead he was hardly given the chance of two successive internationals until Bobby Robson persevered with him a year before Mexico.

The 13th World Cup, La Copa del Mundo, should have resolved the Hoddle dilemma. The setting was perfect for him to display his special talents at the highest level, but on the occasion his performances were inconclusive and will allow the discussions about his true value to continue unabated. Ineffective, together with his team-mates, against Portugal and Morocco, Glenn began to shine against Poland, when he was involved in all three Gary Lineker goals. He was outstanding against Paraguay, creating all three England goals, two more for Lineker and one for Peter Beardsley.

The turning-point for Hoddle in the World Cup was a mixture of farce and fortune. Ray Wilkins' stupidity in managing to get himself sent off in a fit of pique and frustration shortly before half-time against Morocco worked in Hoddle's favour. Immediately England re-organised, Hoddle assuming his familiar central midfield role, and his flair for the creative long ball began to become evident in the second half against the African team that was hailed the surprise of the World Cup. With Peter Reid installed as Wilkins' replacement against Poland, Hoddle had more freedom in the next two games, but unfortunately he was vastly overshadowed by Maradona in the quarter-final tie.

But Hoddle, at 30, still hopes to play in the World Cup finals in Italy in 1990. Perhaps then he will prove once and for all that he is England's most gifted player. Since the first edition of *Spurred to Success* was published in the spring of 1987, Hoddle, who has the perfect attributes for the Continental style of play, has fulfilled his ambition to play abroad. Spurs Chairman Irving Scholar granted his move to Monaco – just reward for his sterling service to the London Club. Hoddle has not regretted this decision – it has given him the opportunity to develop his skills within a system that provides the perfect environment for his special talents.

It has been English football's good fortune that he stayed so long – his departure was a sad loss. I happen to fall into the pro-Hoddle camp. I watched him develop from the age of 17 from the Spurs youth team and reserves through to the senior side. I was there when he scored a spectacular cross-shot goal at Stoke on his Tottenham full debut.

Brian Clough has tried in the past to sign Hoddle for Nottingham Forest. He's a committed Hoddle fan. He says:

'You don't have to bare your false teeth to prove you're a real he-man in football. Some people are morally brave and Hoddle is one of them. I've heard him criticised for non-involvement, but I'm not sure what that means. If you can compensate with more skill in one foot than most players have in their whole body, then that is compensation enough'.

I count myself fortunate to have served my football apprenticeship on the now defunct *North London Weekly Herald*, whose main offices were 150 yards from the White Hart Lane ground. Perhaps inevitably, that has coloured my view. But, from my vantage point in Fleet Street, where one of the golden rules is objectivity, Hoddle represents the embodiment of what I like to see in football: entertainment, skill and originality. Few possess these qualities. Glenn Hoddle is one of them.

Glenn featured prominently in one reviewer's look back at 1986: 'the consensus of opinion among football journalists is that Hoddle is the only player one would pay to watch . . . Hoddle is, simply, a master of his peculiar craft. Other, less gifted players will provide the commitment required by the kind of managers who talk in hundreds of per cent. Nevertheless, it is significant that a large majority of professional footballers regard Hoddle as the nearest thing to the finished football article the English game possesses.

'Can you imagine the First Division without him? I suggest that to lose him would not only be compounding the felony which has robbed us of Lineker and Hughes and will take Rush from us in time, but would create a skill vacuum which may never again be filled. Hoddle is the last of the line of players who will add to the gate at away matches simply by turning up.

'Years ago, supporters of Middlesex would carry their bottles of Tizer to Lord's praying in their heart of hearts that they would be privileged to watch Wally Hammond bat. Now supporters of football go to White Hart Lane praying that today will be one of Hoddle's days, that they will see a performance they can store in the memory banks to be relived by children or grandchildren. Hoddle is one of those players.

'The footballers of tomorrow are no longer those bare-footed kids who kicked a ball of rags between terraced houses pretending to be Matthews, Finney, Skinner, Normanton or Uncle Tom Cobbleigh. They are more discerning now, more sophisticated. They require the best if they are not to be easily bored with football. While a team full of workers may be the modern coach's dream, a team full of Hoddles is their nightmare. Conversely, the latter may be the only true enticement to a public which is currently at best sceptical and at worst scornful.'

Off the field, the Hayes-born player whose only superstition is wearing the No 10 shirt, is quiet, polite, modest and even shy. Throughout his career he has shunned controversy, and declined big-money offers to criticise colleagues and bosses. Here, for the first time, Hoddle tells the real inside story of his life in soccer, of his disagreements with and his personal opinions of the managers he has served under: Bobby Robson, Ron Greenwood, Peter Shreeve, Keith Burkinshaw, Terry Neill and David Pleat.

Never before has he spoken about himself the way he does in this book. His experiences with a faith healer, for example, are quite extraordinary. On one level the healing sessions with Eileen helped overcome numerous injuries, and may have even saved his career. On a higher plane, his friendship with this remarkable Harlow woman played a part in changing his entire life. His account of events in Mexico, where he was a central character, are related with humour, offering a unique insight into the England camp under Robson. His warnings to youngsters hoping to make their way in the professional arena about the pitfalls make fascinating reading. Glenn's conception of a Superleague and his views on the major topics in football such as hooliganism provide a new insight into a player who might, one day, possess managerial qualities.

This is not the autobiography of a bitter man with grudges

against managers or players. It is not in his nature to be outspoken just for the sake of it. Yet Glenn Hoddle is controversial, even provocative, in his willingness to discuss frankly a number of problem areas in the game.

'Hod', as they affectionately call him in the Tottenham camp, has won two FA Cup medals, a UEFA Cup medal and a Little World Cup medal with the England youth team. He would like to take England to the World Cup final in Italy in 1990. Now pursuing his career abroad, and with more than a decade of success with Spurs behind him, he has plenty of ambitions left to fulfil. In this new edition of his book, Hoddle has extended his story to provide a personal account of his long-awaited move to the Continent.

This is not an autobiography in the usual sense. Glenn has written as much about the game as about himself. The book explores his significance in the British concept of how the game should be played, and his rebellion against the accepted principles of work-rate first, and skill and individualism second. It has been a crusade, but in Glenn's view, a worthwhile one.

Harry Harris
Croydon
June 1988

1
Mexico Bound

It's easy to be wise after the event. Anyone can dissect the greatest soccer show on earth with the benefit of hindsight. However, before the events of the World Cup unfolded – before Bobby Robson named his squad for Mexico, before the tragic injury to Mark Wright, before all the controversy in Monterrey and the Azteca Stadium – I sat in one of the lounges of Spurs' new luxurious five million-pound stand on a sunny May morning and looked ahead to Mexico . . .

My choice to take on the world would be Peter Shilton, Gary Stevens (Everton), Kenny Sansom, Terry Butcher, Mark Wright, Bryan Robson, Peter Reid, myself, Gary Lineker, Peter Beardsley (or Tony Woodcock), and Chris Waddle. But from my present vantage point I predict that in Mexico the manager will start with Peter Shilton, Gary Stevens, Kenny Sansom, Terry Butcher, Mark Wright, Bryan Robson, myself, Ray Wilkins, Gary Lineker, Mark Hateley and Chris Waddle.

The reason I would choose Peter Reid ahead of Ray Wilkins is, I suppose, a little selfish. It would give the midfield greater balance, as I prefer to play in central midfield rather than wide on the right. I also have my doubts about whether three players in midfield will be able to cope with the extreme heat in Mexico. In my team I would not choose one of the big, traditional English-type centre forwards, like Mark Hateley or Kerry Dixon. I believe it is a myth that the way to overcome foreign opposition is to get the ball into the box and beat them in the air. Continental sides are no longer pushovers in the air. They have subtle ways of blocking off strikers to prevent them from ever reaching the ball. There are ways to avoid that, but I would opt anyway for two small men in England's attack out in Mexico. We will need more flexibility and subtlety up front. I would not abandon the big striker altogether – he would be a valuable option to have available. I would put Mark Hateley ahead of Kerry Dixon, as he has gained valuable experience playing in Italy.

I am looking forward to playing alongside Lineker. We haven't yet had the opportunity of playing together at international level. There was a chance a while ago for my club to buy him. When that possibility was being explored I spoke to Gary on the way home from England duty in Mexico. As we sat on the plane I tried to persuade him to come to Spurs, telling him what a great club it was. I was convinced that Gary and I would hit it off. I'm sure he wanted to come to Spurs. He told me he would love to play for a club like Tottenham, and I assured him that he would enjoy the way Tottenham play the game.

Gary had consistently scored goals at Leicester, and Spurs bid £825,000 for him a year before his contract at Filbert Street expired. Leicester manager Gordon Milne insisted on a million-pound fee. Not even the likes of Liverpool, Everton and Manchester United were willing to spend anything near that sum at that time. But I believe he was worth a million, and that my club should have spent it. That's easy to say now, I know. He had scored 20 goals a season at Leicester, but no one could have known he would notch up 40 in his first season with Everton. If Gary Lineker had scored as often for Spurs and brought us the First Division Championship we have coveted for so long, then, of course, he would have been worth his million pounds. I know we would have had a far more successful season with Gary in our team and, if we had not won something in his first season, undoubtedly top honours would have eventually arrived. I understand the club were prepared to go as high as £900,000 at a time when the top price for a player in a depressed transfer market was around £700,000. There are some special players who are worth the extra money.

I was personally very disappointed when Gary went to Goodison. He is ideal for my style of play – he makes exciting forward runs and I can find him with long-range passes, and he has exceptional speed, which enables him to leave defenders standing.

My best season at Tottenham has been with speedy strikers able to make darting runs into space. Steve Archibald and Garth Crooks were the perfect front men to capitalise on my 40-yard service. They would make sharp, fast, forward runs without even stopping to think about whether I would notice. They knew I was on their wavelength. I told them if they made those sort of bursts I would get the ball through to them, and it worked a treat. This is something I've been trying to instil in Kerry Dixon with England. At first Steve Archibald and Garth Crooks thought I would never be able to get the ball through to them, and it's the same with Kerry. Steve and Garth found out that it can be done.

I have not yet had the chance to prove my theory with Gary. We have not played yet at international level, as I said, we have worked together only at England get-togethers. But I am confident it will work in Mexico, given the chance, and that Gary will score goals. I thought Garth Crooks at his best was quick, but Gary is even faster! I can see Gary doing the business in Mexico. I've got the ability to place my passes accurately beyond defenders, and he has the pace to lose them. If Gary doesn't score in the first or second game, perhaps the manager will try a different attacking strategem, who knows? But as I sit here looking ahead to the World Cup, I feel that Gary will be the man to inflict most damage on the other teams' defences.

Bryan Robson should play – unless his shoulder becomes so bad that it makes it impossible for him to carry on. I like playing alongside Bryan in midfield. He gives me the ball quite a lot. He makes good, penetrating forward runs, perfect for the type of ball I can play to him. Bryan is going to have to be honest with himself when it comes to assessing his fitness for the World Cup finals. Most players are – there is no point in letting down your team-mates or in exposing your own vulnerability if you are not fit enough for the intensity of the action out in Mexico.

Bryan is not the sort of captain who believes his job involves being an exhibitionist, running around shouting his mouth off and making sure the public see him as the leader. At the appropriate moment during a match he will quietly have a word with a team-mate if something needs to be done. That's my sort of captain, not someone who rants and raves for the benefit of enhancing a public image. But that does not mean he is a softie, far from it. He will give a colleague a fierce lecture if he merits one, but at the same time, he will give praise where it is due.

I have to be given the responsibility of playing in central midfield to bring the best out of my game and to make me as effective as possible for England's cause. When Ray Wilkins is in the England team I am shoved out wide on the right side of midfield, and that doesn't suit me at all. Nor, I think, does it suit the England team. I want to be more involved – I need to be more involved. But that does not necessarily mean that Ray and I cannot play together in the same midfield. We both have good footballing brains and we have played together now for a number of years. In fact, I have a lot of respect for Ray both as a player and as a person. He suffered a torrid time at Manchester United before moving to AC Milan for £1.5 million. He was even called 'The Crab' by his own manager, Ron Atkinson. But he managed to survive all the trauma, and that's an object lesson for all players. Ray is a smashing guy.

If the manager wants me to play wide on the right side of midfield in Mexico, that is where I shall play. But I am sure in the heat of the game there will be plenty of opportunities to drift a little more into the middle, and that is where I will be able to perform to the best of my abilities, and to be most effective for my country.

The England set-up has another smashing player in Chris Waddle. Sometimes he can get bogged down on the left flank – I feel he is a better player on the right wing. He has all the ability in the world, but there are times when he feels sorry for himself, particularly when things are not going his way. If anything goes wrong, it's like the start of World War Three. But, as I keep telling him, if he makes mistakes he shouldn't worry. My advice to Chris has always been not to allow anything to affect him or to deter him. He's learning all the time and doesn't worry as much as he used to. He is a quiet Geordie, and we are close friends off the field which, I suppose, is only natural as we are Tottenham team-mates. We enjoy the same sort of pastimes, such as music, and we go out together with our wives. When you do get to know him, you discover that he has a dry sense of humour, and he can be hilarious at times. His Geordie accent is like something out of *Auf Wiedersehen Pet*, and his north-eastern phrases have me in stitches. You can hear him during a game cursing to himself when he plays a bad ball or something goes wrong. 'Choppers!', he will say under his breath, which, roughly translated, means 'Oh, sod it'. If something goes badly wrong it's 'Monster choppers'!

I first met Chris on England duty, and as with Gary Lincker I urged him to join Tottenham. I'm glad he took my advice. He has special abilities and will one day prove his world class.

Kenny Sansom might be a deadly rival on the pitch as one of the 'opposition' from across North London, but we have been close friends for many years, and we are England room-mates. Kenny is the England football team's great comic. He is a simply brilliant mimic. His impersonations of Prince Charles and Norman Wisdom are his star turns. If we are having a drink after a game, he will stand up and put on a show. It is quite an experience sharing a room with him – he gets me at it, and before long we are both rolling about in stitches.

Kenny has a great knack for picking things up. For

instance, after watching the film *Greystoke*, we went back to our room and he turned into a monkey, making ape noises and jumping all over the beds. I'm sure he could make it in showbusiness. As for me, I never stop singing. I always take my Walkman and tapes away with me and I am happy. We sit in our room while on England duty, me singing to myself and Kenny practising one of his impersonations – neither of us can get to sleep. Just think, I will have seven weeks of Kenny Sansom . . .

The one player I would like to see included in Bobby Robson's World Cup side, but I'm sure will not be, is Paul Walsh. The manager has a fair idea of the squad he will be taking to the World Cup finals, and while we are all sweating on whether or not it includes us, Paul Walsh doesn't even appear to be in the reckoning. Yet Paul has extra special abilities in the opposition's penalty box that I'd like to see utilised in Mexico. When I first played with him for England I thought he was a greedy player, and when he was at Luton he looked as though he could always be pushed aside off the ball. But since he joined Liverpool they have brought the best out of him, and now he does the right things at the right time.

The England manager, Bobby Robson, has his good points. He has a broad knowledge of the game, and in terms of motivation he knows how to get the best out of individuals. But he finds it difficult to relate to his players. His greatest annoyance is being unable to gather his players around him the day after an international to discuss the problems and try to sort them out. His frustrations build up because he cannot talk with his players as a group for long periods between England games. Instead of analysing a performance he spends the morning after the night before talking with the Press, when he would rather be with his players. At club level, the manager can sit down with a player and get to know him. That does not happen in the England set-up. Being with his players for seven weeks on World Cup duty will give the England manager the opportunity to get closer to his players, and perhaps a few of the barriers will be broken down. I am not suggesting that he should become their bosom pal, but at long last he will get to know us a lot better as personalities, as individuals, as people.

I am not questioning Bobby Robson's ability as England manager. He has a sound football brain, even exceptional talents. Many players might not agree with me – and he has had his fair share of critics – but I respect and rate him highly. He is very patriotic, and he loves his job, despite all the sniping and backstabbing that goes with it. He regards the England team as 'my boys' when he sends us out to play for our country. In comparison with Ron Greenwood he is not easy to talk to, although on a one-to-one level it is easier to relate to Bobby, he relaxes more. But if you bumped into Ron Greenwood in the corridor of the hotel, he would stop and talk to you about any topic.

It is this failure of Bobby's to really communicate with his players that has caused me a great deal of personal concern and even anxiety prior to the selection of the final 22 for Mexico. In fact, the build-up to the World Cup has been fraught for us all, or at least for the majority of players in Bobby Robson's squad. The uncertainty over final selection for the World Cup 22 is the reason, I believe, behind the nervousness among several players in games leading up to the final choice. That anxiety has caused disappointing performances in parts of the world where the nation would have expected an England team to overwhelm the opposition, such as Egypt and Israel.

Apart from a small nucleus of players such as Peter Shilton, Bryan Robson and Kenny Sansom, no one is positive of inclusion. Of course, we have a fair idea, and our expectations are high. But I feel it would have made much more sense to have told at least 16 or 17 players that they are certain to be on the plane to Mexico, barring, of course, unforeseen events such as serious injury.

There is a big doubt in my mind about whether I will be going to the World Cup finals. It might sound as though I am a little lacking in confidence at the moment, but that is not the case. The media, and people inside the game and my club are sure I will be selected. But that doesn't make it any easier to cope with the uncertainty in the back of my mind. My uncle, Dave Hoddle, rang me for a chat before the Israel game and as the conversation got around to the World Cup, he asked me how I was looking forward to Mexico. I told him I wasn't even sure of going! He was shocked.

When the England squad got together before those vital build-up games, you could see the worry in the eyes of the other players. I am sure the uncertainty has got to Alvin Martin in particular. He seemed to be very nervous knowing he was playing for a place. It was hard enough for players such as myself; it must have been a nightmare for someone like Alvin whose place is even less secure.

The World Cup is the biggest stage in world football and my ambition is to play there and play well and my hope is that England can win the tournament. I would like to score goals, of course, but to create them would also give me enormous satisfaction. I cannot say that the World Cup is my chance to prove something – I have nothing to prove to anyone other than myself.

Ron Greenwood put a question-mark against my name in the last World Cup in Spain. He didn't feel it was right to pick me at that time, and I only played one and a half games in 1982. But since the summer tour of Mexico in 1985 I have been a regular in Bobby Robson's team. It is a relief that I am no longer under the pressure of 'Hoddle's last chance' rumblings before every England game I play these days. I am not under any delusions that I will go to Mexico to win the World Cup on my own. I believe we have some very good players quite capable of making an impact in Mexico. We also have an amazing team spirit. Off the field the lads get on so well, my particular personal friends being Kenny Sansom and Chris Waddle. Gary Lineker and I are involved in a timeshare scheme that gives us the use of a villa in Spain. The Harrington Grange company allow us three weeks a year each at the villa. We have this arrangement, together with a number of personalities in snooker and horse racing, for a 32-year period.

I am very patriotic, and I have always supported the England team. I remember crying my eyes out when England won the World Cup in 1966. I was eight at the time, and my friend Andy Jessey and I made a huge banner which we paraded around the streets of Harlow. Afterwards I stuck it in my window. It read: 'England for the World Cup'. Not very original!

I believed then that England could win the World Cup and I believe we can win it now. My favourites would be Argentina, Brazil, France, Denmark, Mexico, Uruguay and ourselves. I am sure the 1986 World Cup will be one of the most unpredictable ever. Usually, a team comes through during the tournament, and the team bang on form leading up to it does not generally go on to win. That is the only thing that worries me about England. We have done so well in the year coming up to the finals, and I am a firm believer that a winning streak has to come to an end some time. I still have a sneaking feeling for England, though. We have the best team spirit I have ever known in an international squad.

The slower pace of play we are expecting in the heat of Mexico will suit me. I'm sure I will get more time on the ball and more space to use it. It will not be like the helter-skelter of the English First Division where the game is played at 100 miles an hour. That won't be humanly possible. It is a great advantage to have been on the tour of Mexico last year. We know we have nothing to fear from the altitude and the heat, and we also know that the greater enemy of the two will be the heat. If I am chosen, I will be going out there in optimistic mood for the nation and for myself. At the age of 28, I should be at my peak, and I also feel I have had my best-ever season in the First Division in terms of consistency. My club has not performed as well as we would have wished, but although it has been a very disappointing season for the club, it was not for me personally in terms of performance.

My anxieties about my World Cup place were ended when the squad gathered for the last international before the finals. We knew then that we would be going to Mexico. Bobby Robson told the players who had gathered for the Scotland match that their places were assured, although there were still one or two tickets up for grabs.

The FA sent a registered letter to all the players chosen confirming details of the arrangements, accommodation and suchlike. On the actual day the FA announced the England squad for Mexico I first learned about it when I got home and turned on Teletext!

World Cup fever struck long before touchdown in Colorado Springs where we spent our acclimatisation period. It began to bite when the England squad got together for our final build-up international against Scotland. At our normal headquarters at an hotel in Buckinghamshire, a professor lectured the squad on what we should eat and drink to help us to cope with the conditions we would experience in Mexico. The players are not the greatest of listeners, but everyone was paying close attention. In fact we asked a number of questions, particularly about diet and altitude. We used high-energy drinks all the time during training, and we were told that because of the danger of dehydration in the excessive heat and humidity we had to keep drinking until we reached the point where we would automatically remember to drink without being prompted by thirst.

For the first time I changed my eating habits. Like the rest of the squad I adopted a high-carbohydrate diet leading up to a game. It was pasta all the way, lasagne and spaghetti, and honey and chocolate were a favourite on the day of a game. Huge skips were filled with a few little delicacies for the lads when we flew out to Colorado – HP sauce, mustard, tins of beans and Mars bars by the case. Personally, I am particularly fond of chocolate.

The England-Scotland game was almost overshadowed by the final details of the preparations for the World Cup trip. For that reason it must have been the most relaxed match between the 'auld enemies' I can remember. Normally this fixture is shrouded in tension, but this time the build-up involved such exercises as being fitted for our World Cup suits, and posing for photographs for Mexico, and on the day of the game everyone felt quite good and totally relaxed. To cap it all, we had a good result – a 2–1 victory to take the Sir Stanley Rous Cup – and I scored England's second goal with a header.

The only problem was the handful of League commitments to be fulfilled before we left for Colorado, and the major fear was that someone would sustain a serious injury. Mark Wright was a certainty for Mexico, but a terrible collision with his own goalkeeper, Peter Shilton, in the FA Cup semi-final with Liverpool resulted in a broken leg, a tragedy for the lad. I cannot say I consciously held back in the final few games I played for my club, but I certainly prayed before going out on to the pitch that I would come off it safely. In fact, as it turned out, I hit really good form in the final stages of the season, which was very important to me – I wanted to go to the World Cup on top of my game.

Coincidentally, one of Spurs' final games of the season was a testimonial for our great Argentinian World Cup star Ossie Ardiles, a player I greatly admire and who has helped me enormously since he arrived in this country after the 1978 tournament with a gold winners' medal. Inter-Milan were the guest team, and turning out for Tottenham was Diego Maradona, Argentina's World Cup captain, who cost Naples a world-record six million pounds in transfer fees. Testimonials are generally no more than exhibition matches, but this game was something more than that. It was competitive, not strolling, and proved to be one of the most enjoyable games I have played in for a long time.

Naturally, the sheer magnetism of Maradona lifted the atmosphere. A staggering 30,000-plus crowd turned up for the match, and the kick-off had to be delayed for 15 minutes to allow thousands of fans who had been stranded outside in the late rush to get in. Maradona and Ossie entered the stadium after the two teams to thunderous applause. It was clear that the public were enthralled to have the chance to see a player of Maradona's special skills, and he didn't disappoint them. Of course he did not extend himself to the full, but I am a player whose philosophy is built around skilful football, and I could not but admire this stocky little genius.

Ossie had told Maradona all about me before the game. Ossie has always rated me highly and has said in interviews that he believes my technique is nearer to the South American style than that of any other player he has come across in this country. The *Mirror* newspaper had organised, through Ossie, an exclusive interview with Maradona, and their photographer Monte Fresco, one of the funniest men in Fleet Street, arrived at White Hart Lane before the kick-off to take photographs of Maradona with me. That gave me the chance to meet him for the first time. I couldn't speak Spanish and he didn't know a word of English, but we crossed the language barrier when we were on the same pitch as team-mates. Ossie told me later that Maradona had said to him after the match that he had enjoyed playing with me. That certainly made me feel extremely proud.

When we confronted each other in very different circumstances in Mexico, Maradona had not forgotten me. As we stood in the tunnel in the magnificent Azteca Stadium before the World Cup quarter-finals he caught my eye as the teams lined up, winked and put up his thumb in a sign of acknowledgement. I was pleased by that gesture, but I was also looking out for him.

At this particular stage of England's build-up everyone I met was wishing me luck. The World Cup was now on everybody's minds. It was gratifying to know that the country was behind you, but it was also very frightening to realise that the nation's aspirations were resting on your shoulders. The pressure was on, but at the same time it was a good feeling to be involved. Now I was hyped up and raring to go. The squad met up at the Post House at Heathrow and we were off to high altitude training and acclimatisation to heat in Colorado.

Our headquarters in Colorado were the Broadmoor Hotel. The hotel was sheer wonderment, it took your breath away. I have travelled the world, one of the greatest perks of professional football, and I have stayed at some of the finest hotels, but none matched the beauty of the Broadmoor. The backdrop was the Rockies, and the building itself was a subtle blend of old-world grace and modern convenience, contemporary comforts blending into Italian Renaissance decor. There were three main dining-rooms, which the hotel proudly boasted were 'three of the world's most famous'. On the walls of the tavern hung original Toulouse-Lautrec lithographs. The facilities included a championship standard 54-hole golf course, a World Arena ice rink, 16 tennis courts, two outdoor swimming pools, shooting grounds and a truly magnificent lake. The entire complex was vast. We were told that an Englishman had come to Colorado and had built the hotel in 1918 to remind him of home. Its reputation for quality and service persists, and it is interesting to read the hotel's brochure: 'Attire – The recreational activities of the Broadmoor dictate informal attire and sportswear during the day. In the evenings, after 6pm gentlemen wear coat and tie in the Penrose Room, Charles Court and the Main Dining-Room. Coat or jacket is appropriate in The Tavern. Ladies will want to wear dresses and suits'. Despite the very hot days, the doormen wore the most elaborate top hats and tails. Well, you get the feeling of the place. It can be summed up in one word: posh. I don't suppose it has ever before been invaded by an English football team, not to mention the entire Fleet Street football Press corps, and our behaviour was impeccable . . . well, most of the time.

Just once in a while there were a few high jinks. I'm sure if Bobby Robson had spotted us there would have been a few more grey hairs in his head. One day the lads decided to have a golf competition. We all put money into a kitty and the first prize was 60 dollars. I was delighted when I won it – it was the first time I had ever won anything at golf – but my victory was not achieved without a few laughs along the way.

In my group were Kenny Sansom, Mark Hateley and my Tottenham team-mate Gary Stevens. We drove one of the hotel's buggies around the course, and coming up to the 18th hole we were driving downhill far too fast. We went over a bridge with Kenny steering and I had my foot pressed hard down on the accelerator. Kenny was panicking. He kept shouting 'stop, you nut!', but I kept my foot down and we really flew over that bridge. When it seemed as though we were bound to smash into a wall on the other side, Kenny turned the wheel sharply – and fell out! I took over the steering and brought the buggy to rest safely, while Kenny was flat out on his back. If Kenny had injured himself we would have been in deep trouble, but as it was he ended up laughing his head off. At first I was a bit concerned but when I saw that he was giggling, I couldn't help but laugh too. I am quite sure the manager wouldn't have seen the funny side of it. And to cap it all, out little accident happened beside the 18th green, in full view of the members' clubhouse!

It was episodes such as these that helped us to take our minds off the pressure of the games ahead. They also helped to relieve some of the boredom of being stuck in the same place with the same blokes for so long. That wasn't the only time we had a few laughs on the golf course. The wives came out to the Broadmoor for a week, and while in some quarters that was frowned upon the players welcomed the arrival of the girls. After all, we were going to be together for seven weeks. That is an awful long time, and even though Kenny and myself are great pals, it is too long a period to spend in such close proximity to one another. But because we are known to be such good friends, when the girls arrived, we claimed that we still wanted to stay together in our room. As a joke, we showed Kenny's wife Elaine and my wife Anne to 'their' room. I'm sure at first they believed us!

We had another game of golf when our wives were with us, and this time we were perfectly safe in the buggies. Anne drove our buggy, Elaine drove for Kenny, and Lorna, Chris Waddle's wife, drove for 'Widdley'. Now 'Widdley' doesn't play too much golf, and he was hitting the ball anywhere except where he was aiming. Anne took a snap of us all hiding behind one of the buggies as 'Widdley' shaped up to play a shot.

The spirit among the lads was phenomenal – there wasn't a single row or disagreement for the entire duration of the trip. Although it may sound a whole lot of fun, I can assure you that the preparation was thorough and was very hard work. The medical staff took tests at sea level on pulse rate, haemoglobin levels and recovery rate, which were repeated at altitude. Every day we were weighed, our temperatures were taken and our fluid levels measured. We were losing pounds after every training session.

The day after the England squad arrived in Colorado the doc, Vernon Edwards, said we would be going for a 'leisurely walk'. This turned out to be an upward hike of 10,000 feet towards Pike's Peak. That took some effort so soon after arriving in Colorado. Fortunately, we didn't quite go all the way to the summit, which was an extra 4,000 feet. The climb was bad enough, the road was narrow with a sheer drop at some bends, but coming down, a few of us decided that we couldn't be bothered to walk. Instead, we ran. That was some run. It was very scary, to say the least. In fact, I took a tumble and badly cut my arm. It could have been worse, and that would not have pleased the manager.

The initial hard graft was done at the Academy, an army training and recreational complex about a half an hour's coach ride from the hotel, and like most facilities in the States it was impressive. After every training session we would have 15 minutes in the steam room – if you could last that long – to acclimatise to the humid conditions we would experience in Monterrey. Then it was 15 minutes in the sauna, and a shower. The centre also had a huge swimming pool, and most of the lads enjoyed a dip.

As part of the army training, the swimming pool has a very

high diving board. We were passing the pool one day and an army guy was standing up there, unable to pluck up enough courage to leap off the board. We hung around for about a quarter of an hour, until the coast was clear, and a few of the lads climbed up just to see how high it really was. Viv Anderson was the first to jump off, followed by Terry Butcher and Chris Woods. Kenny Sansom, however, saw how high it was and walked back. Then he changed his mind and went to the edge again, but once more he went back. Obviously, he didn't like the look of it, and who could blame him. He must have gone to the edge and back a dozen times – the performance seemed to go on for about half an hour. We were all urging him to jump, and in the end he leaped off.

The next stage of our build-up involved games against World Cup hosts Mexico in Los Angeles and Canada in Vancouver. The travelling was arduous, but it was felt that we needed to maintain match fitness and sharpness. It was a stratagem not adopted by other competing nations. Each game brought an injury problem. First our skipper Bryan Robson hurt his shoulder again against Mexico and failed to finish the game. He dislocated the shoulder joint, but the boss decided to keep this quiet. At this point, I have no doubt that Bobby Robson had to make a decision either to take Bryan Robson on to Mexico or to send him home. I don't think it took the manager long to reach the conclusion that he would be better off taking the skipper. If he had been only, say, 60 per cent fit, then I felt we would have been better off without him, but the fact was that he was very close to fitness. The risk was always there that, should he fall on the elbow or the shoulder, he would dislocate the shoulder again. The risk was the same before we left England. Bryan is a great player, world class, and if he was fit, he should have been in the side.

However, I did not agree with the opinion that if Bryan Robson had been taken out of the England side we would have had no chance in the World Cup. A team ready to challenge the world requires 11 good players. Perhaps we would have been worse off had Peter Shilton been injured, or even Gary Lineker. In fact we nearly lost Gary when he was injured in Vancouver.

I was running behind Gary when he crashed to the ground in a tackle with Randy Samuel, and I heard something crack. My first thought was that something had gone in Gary's groin region. In fact, he had cracked a tiny bone in his wrist. In the first few training sessions in Monterrey he looked very unbalanced with the heavy strapping on his wrist. He was clearly apprehensive. I considered Gary very fortunate to have maintained his fitness sufficiently to enable him to play in the World Cup. Had it been a main bone in the wrist he surely wouldn't have made it. As it turned out we were all very grateful that Gary Lineker did manage to participate in the World Cup.

2
The World Cup 1986

Now we were in Mexico at last and the opening game wasn't far away. My Tottenham team-mate Gary Stevens, Peter Beardsley and Alvin Martin found it very difficult to breathe at first, but the rest of the squad knew what to expect as a result of our experience in Mexico the previous summer. I'm sure our knowledge of the conditions gave us a phsycological advantage.

Before the opening match with Portugal there was an air of expectancy in our temporary home, the out-of-the-way Camino Real Hotel an hour's coach-drive from Monterrey. Situated nearly 100 miles up the mountain in Saltillo, we were virtually cut off from the rest of civilisation. At first it was hard to get used to, but soon we came to realise that the peace of our mountain retreat was an absolute necessity. A convoy of cars and trucks would accompany the team coach through the winding mountain passes down the hill to Monterrey to the Sima Club. The players had never experienced heat conditions like it. Training was a real sweat.

But everyone was keyed up for the chance to have a go at Portugal. There was a belief that England could win the World Cup – we had watched some of the opening games on television together and there was absolutely nothing that frightened us. Confidence was sky-high. We did not play particularly brilliant football against Portugal but we were not that bad. With a little luck we would have won comfortably. Instead we were caught with a sucker punch. Portugal scored late in the game, causing what was probably the biggest upset thus far in the World Cup. It was even harder to comprehend for the rest of the world considering the incredible problems Portugal had suffered during their build-up to the competition. In the week leading up to the start of the 1986 World Cup finals, Portugal were in such a state of disarray that their team, led by veteran goalkeeper and captain Bento, threatened to strike. An internal row over World Cup bonus payments, the quality of the opposition in the build-up to the finals, and the players' cut from sponsorship money had ripped through the Portugal camp. Ironically, their hotel headquarters, El Torres, were on the other side of the road from our own Camino Real.

On Monday 3 June, in the Estadio Technológico, a defensive error cost us a goal. My room-mate Kenny Sansom was almost inconsolable. He had been beaten by the winger whose cross produced the winner at the far post. Kenny blamed himself, badly, and he was worried. I tried to talk to him. I told him it had been his only mistake in the game, that anyone was entitled to make an error, and that he shouldn't blame himself for what had happened next. He was not the last defender – three others were in a position to do something about it, but no one did. Terry Butcher and Terry Fenwick were unable to cut out the cross, while Gary Stevens allowed the goalscorer to escape him. I brought Kenny round. He needed cheering up, so a little later we went to a reception organised by one of the boot sponsors at the hotel. It was not one of the happiest receptions, but I don't think we were as depressed as the people back home.

Television and the media in general are powerful moulders of public opinion. We knew we would be taking some stick, but the beauty of our mountain retreat was that we were oblivious to it all at the time. I believe that was extremely valuable in helping us to maintain our concentration. We had gone into the World Cup with victories against Mexico and Canada stretching our unbeaten run to almost a year. Somehow that scared me more than anything else. No team can keep on winning indefinitely – one day they will be tripped up. Unfortunately, it happened to us when we really could have done without it, in the opening game of the World Cup finals. Yet it could have been far worse. This was not the knockout stage, we had another chance, and we aimed to take it. As a team we knew we had not become bad overnight. The fact that we had lasted a year unbeaten, and had enjoyed some notable successes in that time, gave us plenty of encouragement.

Back we went to the Estadio Technológico on Friday 6 June for another four o'clock kick-off. At home they were no doubt thinking that if we couldn't beat Morocco we should all be shot. We felt the same way. The resultant goalless draw was hardly going to satisfy the fans, let alone our critics, who were now getting stuck into their task of tearing us apart with a will. We returned to our 'desert island'. Now, we knew, the flak really would be flying. Yet we also knew that it was not *that* bad a result against Morocco. The fact that we had played the entire second half with only ten men and had still come out with a point meant we had a chance in the final match in our group against Poland, the seeded team.

The millions watching the action on their television sets could see the sun was shining, they knew it was hot, but they simply didn't appreciate just how stamina-sapping the conditions were. We gritted our teeth in the face of adversity against Morocco. We stuck to our task and the point we earned ultimately proved to be very valuable. I am sure that if we had had to fly back to England to see and hear for ourselves the severe criticism, and then had had to fly back to tackle Poland, morale would have been so low that we would certainly have lost. We didn't see a newspaper until days after it was published, and even then we didn't take too much notice. We didn't know what was being said on television or radio. We were a group of 22 players cocooned in Saltillo, and grateful for it.

The only knowledge of the reality back in England came from the Press corps and television teams sharing out hotel. Their presence made things a little more difficult than they needed to be. I think it would have been better had they been in a different hotel. A World Cup should be kept very private for the players. There was always a suspicion that the Press might take advantage of the intimacy brought about by sharing the same hotel. Even worse, some of the Press lads kept pinching our sun beds once they had filed their copy first thing in the morning, which was mid-afternoon back in England. Steve Curry of the *Daily Express* was one of the worst culprits. He never missed a chance to sunbathe. Not only was he among the first to the sun beds, he would also borrow my tapes!

The five days between the Portugal and Poland games were agonising. It was the most distressing period for manager Bobby Robson. Everything was thrown up into his face at once. Was he right to have persisted with Bryan Robson? The fact that the England skipper had been taken off minutes before Ray Wilkins was sent off weighed heavily against the manager's decision. I could sense there was a lot of pressure on Bobby Robson. The manager had been very relaxed in team meetings before the first two games. Not so now. He had taken the full force of the flak back home, and he was the man at the helm. But, all credit to the manager, he tried not to let his personal fears get through to the players. He never lost control, he never lost his temper, he never lost his self-respect, even though I'm sure he was on a short fuse with some of the media.

The Sunday newspapers were full of stories about revolt among the players. There was an accusation that skipper Bryan Robson and vice-captain Ray Wilkins had complained to the manager after the final training session before the Morocco game that the players had been worked too hard. There was a suggestion, too, that player-power was behind the change in tactics. That was also sheer fantasy. There were no internal rifts between the players. There were no troubles between the players and the manager. Training before the Morocco match was hard and it was sharp, but it was no slog in the sun. There was an open discussion about the length of that training session, and it was the manager who asked the players if they were feeling the heat. There was nothing special about that. Bobby Robson asked the players' opinions about the training a few times during the trip. This particular day Ray Wilkins said that, speaking personally, he did feel a little jaded and that he thought we ought to slow down a bit. There were days when I felt we should have relaxed more in training and had a 15-minute five-a-side, by way of a change and as a means of conserving energy.

Bobby Charlton, a star of England's 1970 World Cup team in Mexico, openly criticised the manager's training schedules. He said that Alf Ramsey had not trained his players so hard in the excessive Mexican heat in 1970. He was worried that we were giving too much on the training pitch and didn't have sufficient energy for the actual matches. The medical advice was that we needed to train very hard for 90 minutes each day in the heat. We would work for 45 minutes, stop for a drink, and then carry on for another 45 minutes. The lads thought this was hard work at first, and it was, but the training did ease off as we got closer to the games. Bobby Charlton's views were not a criticism of the players, but they were a criticism of the management and I'm sure Bobby Robson didn't appreciate it.

To make matters worse, Bobby Charlton, in his capacity as a director of Manchester United, wanted Bryan Robson sent back home for an immediate shoulder operation to ensure that he would be fit for the start of Manchester United's season in August. Bobby Robson was not very happy with that suggestion. It would have been terrible for Bryan had we reached the World Cup final itself and he was sitting at home watching it on television. If it had been me, after playing in all those qualifying games and the opening two matches I would have wanted to remain with the England squad. Bobby Charlton may have had the best motives for making his opinions public, but they did not help England's cause. He was out of order.

The whole pattern of England's play was switched after

the Morocco game. When Ray Wilkins was sent off against Morocco, I moved from the right side of midfield to the centre, to the more familiar role in which I play for my club. I felt that was my best position and against Morocco I felt that it showed. I am able to run the midfield from that position and I thought I had a greater influence at the start of the second half against Morocco. But in the final 20 minutes I came up against a strange physical and mental barrier. The last five minutes were the worst. There I was, at the World Cup finals, and yet I was running from memory. I had not so much a pain, more an ache in every part of my body. It was like having the 'flu, when all your strength and willpower drains away. Afterwards I found I had lost eight and a half pounds in that one match.

I am a great believer in fate. A new-look England team, with Peter Reid in a four-man midfield, was selected for the Poland game, and it suited me perfectly. For my Tottenham team-mate Chris Waddle and good friend Mark Hateley, however, it wasn't such good news. They were dropped. Chris was in urgent need of a lift. I didn't have the chance to sit down with him and have a long chat, but I spoke to him about the situation. He went over on his ankle in a training session just before the Poland game, which wouldn't have helped his chances of selection. But he was fit enough to play, and he had been left out. He took it really well. The manager assured us that Chris was not the scapegoat nor the excuse to switch to another system. Bobby Robson insisted that Chris played well against Portugal, and he did. I knew Chris, like Mark Hateley, was disappointed, but what can you say? I just told him that he had been unlucky and that he must keep going and not sulk. Situations in football have a habit of changing rapidly. He had to consider himself part of the squad. With that attitude he made more appearances as substitute than might have been the case if he had allowed his head to drop.

I knew what it was like to be left out of a World Cup team. It had happened to me in 1982 in Spain. I managed to play only one and a half games. So I knew what Chris was going through, and it wasn't easy to cheer him up. But to emphasise the strength of the team spirit within the squad, none of the players left out let their depression get through to the other lads. No one transmitted any negative feelings – everyone wanted England to win, including those players who had been left out. That's what made it such a good squad. Bryan Robson and Ray Wilkins were magnificent. They shared a room and it must have been a sanctuary for them from all the problems. But in front of the lads they put on a brave face.

The mood of the players before the Poland match was one of calm. Bobby Robson's team talk for this match took on a new significance. We all knew we had to win, otherwise we would be out of the World Cup. 'It's all down to you, lads', he told us. He talked more about our opponents, Poland, than he had done when we faced Portugal and Morocco. I always feel that's a giveaway sign of tension.

I was delighted that we had switched to the Estadio Universitario. I didn't like the stadium in which we played our first two games – it was like a college pitch, there was no atmosphere, and it just did not feel as though we were actually taking part in the World Cup finals. Behind one goal, where we changed, there was no stand, and to top it all the pitch was in a poor state. The move to the second stadium in Monterrey was a godsend. From a personal point of view I was much happier playing in the middle of midfield alongside Peter Reid. We had played well together the previous summer in the final two games of our tour: we have contrasting styles that complement each other.

Gary Lineker's three quick and excellent goals resulted in a win over Poland and qualified us for the eighth finals. Remarkably, it was the unfancied Morocco who topped our group and stayed in Monterrey to play West Germany, but the important thing was that we had qualified. The players greeted the victory with a mixture of relief and pride. Back home, we later discovered, they were dancing in the streets! What an incredible turnaround! Before the Poland match the players and the management had been pilloried: now we were heroes. We deserved our win over Poland, but back in the dressing-room after the match you could almost see the tension lifting from everybody involved with the England party. The players didn't show too much emotion, but the result had raised our spirits and helped to make the entire trip more pleasurable.

We packed our bags and headed for the capital city. At first we had some problems with our accommodation: the hotel was noisy, some of the lads didn't have hot water in their rooms, and there were a few complaints about the general standard of the facilities. So before we played Paraguay we switched to the hotel near the airport, which we shared with the defeated Italian team who were making their way home.

These minor problems did not upset us – England went on to record another fine victory against Paraguay. Many experts rated Paraguay one of the best teams in South America: the new Brazil, some said. For the first 15 minutes of our first game in the Azteca Stadium, the match could have swung either way. Paraguay had a couple of good chances which, had they taken them, would have given them a grip on the game. I enjoyed the Paraguay game more than any other in the World Cup. It was my best game. I had a hand in all three goals, and that was naturally very satisfying.

My only disappointment was the state of the Azteca pitch. On television it must have looked immaculate, but the grass was far too long. In fact Peter Shilton made an official complaint about the goalmouths after this match and something was done to rectify the situation before we played Argentina.

A lot of searching questions were asked before we played Argentina. It was, for a start, the first football match between the nations since the Falklands War. Right from the outset the players were told not to get involved with the political implications. None of the England team did, and nor was there any extra motivation because of the situation. We were very tense before the game and it showed in the opening half, but that tension certainly wasn't caused by worrying about the Falklands or about an episode in history that had occurred four years before!

The ineffectiveness of the England side in the first half was the result of stifling tactics by Argentina. They had changed their team, deploying a defensive midfield player in place of an attacker. The tactics worked, we played into their hands, not getting into the game even though we had a lot more of the ball. Peter Shilton was hardly tested apart from a few crosses and free kicks. There were no real, clear-cut chances; it was undeniably an uninspired, ordinary game for the first 45 minutes.

We made the mistake of playing much longer passes than we had against Poland and Paraguay. Instead of playing through the midfield, the four defenders tried long balls forward to Gary Lineker and Peter Beardsley. Peter Reid and I wanted the ball in midfield. We were becoming frustrated by the lack of service, and I spoke to Terry Butcher and Terry Fenwick, asking for the simple pass to Peter or myself. We kept on needlessly, foolishly conceding possession with our long ball strategy. It simply wasn't working.

We sorted out our problems at half-time. Then, just when we began to really get going at the start of the second half, that infamous handball incident involving Diego Maradona occurred. When the ball flew into the air off Steve Hodge's boot I was about six yards from the referee, watching the action from a similar angle.

I know what I felt about the incident then, and I feel the same way now. I'll never change my mind. I saw Maradona punch the ball in. Some of the players confessed to me later that they had missed it, and didn't really know what had happened until they had seen the action replay on television. But I actually *saw* Maradona's hand go up and punch the ball. I must admit he tried to disguise it very well, flicking his head at the same time as he handled. But it hadn't fooled me. I have seen that done in Sunday morning matches at the local park, and the players there have never got away with it.

But in Mexico, in a World Cup quarter-final, here was an official who shouldn't have been trusted even with a Sunday morning match. I don't blame Diego Maradona, I blame the Tunisian referee, Ali Bennaceur. I saw the referee look over to his linesman, turn and blow his whistle. Incredibly, he pointed to the centre circle indicating a goal.

I felt absolutely sick inside. I chased after him, and as I was running alongside him I pointed to my hand, screaming 'handball!'. It was at this moment I knew, with a sickening feeling in my guts, that the referee hadn't seen it, and that there was no way he would be changing his mind. I looked over to the linesman – perhaps he had seen it, and would be brave enough to draw the referee's attention to the incident. Not at all: the linesman was sprinting back to the halfway line. It was hopeless.

Peter Shilton had also chased halfway down the field to make his protest. He had been, naturally, the nearest player to Maradona and he too knew exactly what had transpired. 'Shilts' seemed determined not to give in – he was protesting so strongly that I feared he might get himself booked or even sent off.

That horrible image of Maradona handling the ball will always remain with me. That nauseating feeling of knowing you have been cheated won't go away either. But how can anyone blame the player? The officials should have spotted the infringement. The best players were at the World Cup finals, but I question whether the tournament had the best officials. Referees were provided by many countries that simply did not merit representation. It is wrong. England should never have been beaten by a goal like that.

Shortly afterwards Maradona scored one of the best individual goals of the entire tournament. That knocked the stuffing out of us. However, we rallied and we were good enough to stage a comeback. Gary Lineker scored and might have got a second goal. We felt we were finishing the game much more strongly, and had we been given the impetus of a second goal we could well have won in extra time. In the latter stages of the match substitute John Barnes and Chris Waddle made a big impact, and we played the best football of the game.

When we trooped back into our dressing-room some harsh words were spoken. I kicked the nearest thing to me, and the air was blue with some of the language. But none of it was directed at Maradona. All players, at some stage of their careers, have flicked a hand out or tried to punch the ball into the goal, more out of cheekiness than an urge to cheat. Few have ever got away with it. Maradona knew he couldn't have got his head to the ball, so he put his hand up. It was an instinctive reaction more than anything else – anyone might have done the same. But no matter how you try to rationalise it, the overriding feeling is one of having been cheated.

Maradona has expressed a desire to come to play football in England. If he still feels like that, and ever realises his wish, I am sure he would carry with him the reputation of the player who cheated England. Although, undoubtedly, the club he signed for and their supporters would welcome him with open arms, I'm not so sure he would enjoy a similar reception from the opposing fans. Eventually, though, I'm sure his superb skills would win everyone over. Personally, I don't hold any grudges against Diego Maradona, but I cannot say I feel the same about the match officials!

When our quarter-final tie was over, Maradona came over to me in the centre of the Azteca Stadium and we embraced. It was a gesture of friendship, and of immediate forgiveness. I wished him good luck for the rest of the competition. He said in Spanish '*Bueno*', meaning 'good'.

The World Cup turned out to be eventful for England, quite a mixture of success and failure, joy and tragedy. On a personal level I believe I played well, and I enjoyed the whole experience. But there was disappointment too – I had felt so sure we would go through to the semi-finals, if not all the way to the final itself. We would be kidding ourselves if we claimed that England had a good World Cup, but in fact we got as far as most experts expected we would get, that is to the quarter-finals. We received a marvellous reaction from the public once we got home, and they made us feel as if we had achieved something. But I was left unfulfilled. We had a great chance to reach the final, and even to win the World Cup, and it had passed by. Yet, somehow it seems wrong to complain. We nearly suffered the unthinkable: the humiliating experience of going out after three games by failing to qualify from the easiest group in the World Cup finals. The pressure was on us to beat Poland and we rose to the occasion. From the jaws of near disaster we beat Paraguay and could have beaten Argentina – and if we had, I don't think we would have failed to reach the final.

There was a lot of character in the team, and that showed up best in the Poland game, and in the latter stages against Argentina.

I would have loved to have scored in the World Cup finals. Perhaps the closest I came to a goal was in the quarter-final tie. After a free kick I raised my arms to celebrate the goal and was astounded by the save from 'keeper Pumpido. It was even more amazing that Gary Lineker failed to score an equaliser. Despite reaching a respectable stage, I still feel as though I have missed out. I didn't really stamp myself on the 1986 World Cup finals. I don't think that is possible unless you go all the way in the competition, or at least to the semi-finals. But I was pleased with the way I played and I enjoyed the entire tournament. It was a terrific experience.

The 1966 World Cup team went all the way to the final, and, of course, eventually won the competition. Members of that team will be remembered as world-class players. But before the finals, some of them, like Roger Hunt, would not have been ranked that highly. Geoff Hurst, too, made his name with a hat-trick in the final itself, yet at the outset Jimmy Greaves was the world's most respected goalscorer. Hurst would not have made such an impact had England been knocked out in the quarter-finals. I do agree, though, that Gordon Banks, Bobby Moore and Bobby Charlton were always world-class performers by anyone's standards.

At the end of the day, I was reasonably satisfied. I would have been less content if I was a player of the calibre of Michael Laudrup. He played three blinders with Denmark and then they flopped.

My only regret is that I felt cheated by the referee against Argentina. When that game was over a powerful depression set in. I felt my last chance to succeed in the World Cup had gone. In the shower after the match, I remember feeling really frustrated. 'The younger players in the team may get another chance,' I thought to myself, 'but this could be it for me.' It was a sorrowful experience. I will be 32 by the time the 1990 World Cup in Italy comes around. But who's to say that England will even qualify? It is possible they will fail. Then that notorious Argentinian game will become my last in the World Cup finals.

But I plan to be around to help England qualify and then my ambition is to be a member of the World Cup squad and to participate in my third World Cup finals. I'm a great believer in that old soccer adage that if you're good enough then it doesn't matter how old you are. That applies to a player of 16 or 17 as well as to a player of 37. You should be selected on merit not according to age. Michel Platini, at 32, was the star of the French team, which contained plenty of players over 30. It is by no means out of the question that I will be involved in 1990, but I shall have to play well for another four years. It is not that easy to maintain top form for a player of my style, and although I'm the only player of my kind in the country at the moment, it is quite possible that some newcomers might emerge in the next three or four years to take my place.

The pace and the endurance required in the First Division makes it tough for a player like myself to survive. It would be interesting to see how many of the top stars from the Continent could cope with the English First Division. It is a hard place for the skilful performer and I'm sure that is one of the factors that puts them off, beside the financial arrangements, of course. Some 40 players have been imported since Ossie Ardiles and Ricky Villa joined Tottenham after the 1978 World Cup finals in Argentina, but only a handful have been top players and precious few have made it.

We flew home from Mexico City the morning after our defeat by Argentina. Bobby Robson stayed to watch the rest of the competition. Anne met me at the airport. It was a very emotional reunion. Someone handed me this baby, and I didn't recognise her – it was my own daughter, Zara Marie. When I set out for the World Cup she was four months old, and now she was six months – I couldn't believe how much she had changed. The reaction from the public was terrific, but the Diego Maradona handball incident played on my mind to such an extent that I would sit at home, trying to relax by watching television, and find I simply couldn't concentrate no matter what the programme.

Several members of the family telephoned to offer their congratulations, and the phone was going non-stop with journalists wanting me to re-live that goal. Re-live it . . . I couldn't stop thinking about it! I was even dreaming about it, although it was more of a recurring nightmare than a dream. For the first time in my football career I didn't want to talk about an incident in the game, not even to close members of my family. I had never felt like that before: normally I love to talk about football. The pressure began to build up, becoming almost unbearable. I felt claustrophobic.

One day, I decided I had just had enough. I said to Anne 'We're going away for a break'. Quickly we fixed up a holiday in Spain. Some friends have a villa there and we decided to join them. The break was just what I needed.

While we were in Spain we went to a German restaurant to watch the World Cup final between Argentina and West Germany. We had heard that the final was to be shown there on a large screen and so off we went. We were recognised and there were a lot of questions about the World Cup and about that Maradona incident, but by now, after a few days relaxing in the sun, the nightmare had receded and I found I could talk about it. The restaurant was jammed, and many of the customers were German. The game began. Matthaeus fouled Maradona and was booked, but the damage was done when the free kick from Jorge Burruchaga was missed by Harold Schumacher and there was centre-half Jose Luis Brown to head home. Silence.

The Germans had conceded the first goal in both the 1954 and 1974 finals and had still gone on to win. In the nine World Cup finals since the Second World War, the team that scored first had lost the game on no fewer than six occasions and the Germans had been involved in three of those. But when Valdano scored the second for Argentina in 1986, I don't imagine many of the Germans in that restaurant packed with some 250 people thought their country stood much of a chance.

In the 73rd minute Voller flicked on a corner for Rummenigge to slide the ball in for his first goal of the entire World Cup tournament. Suddenly the restaurant erupted. With just seven minutes left there came an identical corner from the left. Berthold headed it on and there was Voller in the six-yard box to head it in. It was 2–2 and now the Germans went berserk.

Really, I hadn't taken too much notice of the final until this stage. Now I became more involved. I wanted Argentina to win. I didn't think that the Germans played well in the whole competition and I was surprised that they managed to get to the final playing such mediocre football. The whole world must have thought the final was heading for extra time when the Germans equalised, but a minute later a beautiful pass from Maradona set Burruchaga away, outpacing Briegel and beating the advancing Schumacher. Despite being surrounded by Germans, my mate and I got completely carried away and jumped up shouting 'Yes, get in there! It's a goal!'. We didn't realise that everyone in that restaurant was looking at us in amazement, apart from a couple of Spaniards in the opposite corner who were too busy celebrating themselves. When we noticed how our jubilation was being received, our first reaction was to leave the restaurant as soon as possible! But fortunately there were a lot of families and kids around, and we all had a few laughs about it. It could have been very tricky if the place had been full of yobbos. Nevertheless, after finishing our San Miguel we sneaked out sharpish, just in case!

3
The International Connection

Bobby Robson

Bobby Robson has changed a lot over the five years that I have been playing under him. He's far more relaxed, more in control of his emotions.

When he left Ipswich Town to become manager of England he was uptight about certain situations. He was annoyed by the huge gaps between games during which he was unable to work with his players. His players gathered together for four days at a time between intervals of months, a situation which made him feel frustrated, almost helpless. He found it difficult to adjust to this after being used to a day-to-day involvement with players at club level.

As the years have gone by, I have noticed that Bobby Robson has become more and more positive in whatever he does involving the England team. The World Cup played a big part in helping the England manager to shed his anxieties. The manager and the squad were together for two months, and a tremendous team spirit and harmony was built within the camp that the manager will no doubt want to preserve through the European Championship campaign and on into the 1990 World Cup finals in Italy.

There has always been a good atmosphere between the players and the England officials since I have been a part of the international set-up. But the players and the manager have never been closer than they are now. In the past the players may have held back in what they used to say to the manager, but that is no longer the case. There is a greater ease in the area of communications.

Personally, I owe a great deal to Bobby Robson. He is the England manager who has given my international career the opportunity to really take off. At long last the England manager showed the conviction in my ability to play me virtually non-stop in his side. That is all I have ever asked, and all I have ever wanted.

My biggest regret in international football is that I was deprived of a run of games under Ron Greenwood. It has always baffled me that he decided not to play me after I did well on my debut against Bulgaria. I played in one or two games but never in a real sequence of matches. I feel I should have earned far more England caps than I have done, which is perhaps the principal disappointment of my career. I'm sure I could have been more influential for my country at an earlier age, had Greenwood given me more encouragement.

At the time Bobby Robson became England manager he said that he wanted to build his midfield around me. I was delighted – unfortunately, though, I was injured and so didn't get the chance to play this role early on in his reign. Nevertheless, eventually, once I had regained my fitness, he was as good as his word. I was brought into the team, and I have stayed there. Bobby Robson has been the butt of a lot of criticism, and generally, I feel that much of it is unfair. He is a passionate man, extremely patriotic, and he has a vast knowledge of the game.

He also has a sense of humour, which is fortunate in view of his reputation for getting in a muddle over the odd player's name. One of the funniest such incidents happened during a training session on the playing fields of Bisham Abbey when Watford striker Luther Blissett had just won his place in the England squad.

A group of players, Kenny Sansom, Ray Wilkins and me among them, were standing on the halfway line waiting for our turn in this particular training exercise. The idea was to knock the ball out to a player on the wing, run to join Luther up front, receive a pass from Luther and have a crack at goal. Bobby Robson stood beside our little group while we awaited our part in this attacking ploy. The England manager clearly gestured as if he was about to shout out some vital instruction to Luther. But, instead of bellowing his orders, he turned round, pointing to Luther, and whispered to Ray Wilkins: 'I've forgotten his name, I've forgotten his name!'. Ray supplied the required information. 'Blufer!' yelled a relieved Robson.

The training session came to a complete halt. No one could move for the next two or three minutes – we were all in fits of laughter.

Don Howe

Don Howe is an organised coach, not a defensive coach, and there is a big difference between the two. He is highly organised in the way he wants his teams to play. Quite wrongly, Don has been tarnished with a reputation for approaching his job in a defensive way. He is thought of as a dour and methodical man, rather than as an inspirational character.

The truth is that the public are not aware of one side of Don Howe's personality. He is always in a cheerful mood, he's a superb joke-teller, and he is fond of listening to a good joke. I like him. Yes, Don is a very strict trainer. He makes us work hard, but he appreciates the skilful player, and encourages him to show his ability.

His philosophy is that to be a good team you have to be organised to provide a framework in which the skill factor can blossom. The team pattern is vital if the talented players are to flourish. The old adage in football is that you have to 'fight for the right to play'. Although Don's training is hard, I find it interesting. My only criticism is that perhaps it is *too* strict and a little too short on variety. Since he lost his job at Arsenal, I've sensed that Don has become more relaxed. Now there's a little more fun creeping into his training sessions.

There must have been a great deal of pressure on Don at

Highbury. At the same time he was coaching England and going through the anxieties of getting us ready for the World Cup finals. When he finished at Arsenal you could almost see the burden being lifted from his shoulders. That came through in his training with the England players. He enjoyed himself. True to form, Don trained the players very hard in Mexico, and he was criticised for over-training us. But there was always a reason behind his methods.

I shall always be grateful to Don for helping me at a crucial time in my career. I was being so tightly marked that I was beginning to get stifled by the close attentions of defenders. He sat me down and gave me some good advice about how to counteract tight man-for-man marking. Liam Brady had also suffered in that way because of his ability to open up a match; to create, and score, vital goals. Don said that the best escape was to match force with force, and only after acting on this theory would I be able to free myself to express my full range of skills.

Don opened my eyes. It is unfortunate that it had to be done, but now I have learned to be combative. I'll be truthful – I don't like being shadowed by defenders. Now I deal with it in a positive way: rather than losing faith in my ability to come out on top, I view man-to-man marking as a challenge that I'm determined to overcome.

The England 'team' behind manager Bobby Robson consists of Don as coach, physiotherapists Fred Street and Norman Medhurst, and Dr Vernon Edwards. There is a tremendous amount of work that goes on behind the scenes. Norman and Fred are tireless workers. The doctor is a character, all right. The night before every match he looks into every player's room to see how he is; whether he would like a sleeping tablet; whether there are any little upsets, or any worries. You can hear him when he does his rounds. He has a booming voice, so you know he's coming when he's five doors away!

All the players and indeed everyone connected with the England party was horrified when the doc had a heart attack in Mexico, which was caused by the heat combined with the altitude and the amount of work he was doing. He would be the first to admit he was working too hard for the 'lads'. We all contributed to a whip-round for the doc, and we all signed a gigantic card. He sent us a video from the hospital, recording a message to tell us he would soon be back in the camp. He wanted us to know he was still alive and kicking, and that we shouldn't worry about him and be distracted from our task of trying to win the World Cup for our country.

Terry Venables

I was coached by Terry Venables and Dave Sexton for two years while I played for the England Under-21 team, and I admit it – I'm a Terry Venables fan. Since that time I have often spoken with Terry and I certainly know what he achieved as a manager with Crystal Palace, Queens Park Rangers and Barcelona.

To go to Spain and win the championship in his first season was a magnificent feat. It's hard enough for a player to overcome the language barrier, let alone for a manager, who has to communicate with his players. Not only did Terry adapt to a foreign country, but he also brought with him his own style, converting Barcelona into adopting an English type of game with a typically English back four without the sweeper.

I believe that Terry Venables would bring out the best in me as a player if I worked with him at club level. I have often thought about the prospect of playing for him, and it excites me. Not only would I be keen to play for the club, I'd be keen to play for him.

He is a hard man, and he knows what he wants. Because of the type of player he was with Tottenham, Chelsea, Queens Park Rangers and Crystal Palace, I'm sure he would appreciate how I like to play the game. I wish I had been coached by Terry Venables as a teenager when I was just bursting on to the First Division scene. Terry has the reputation of a 'Crafty Cockney', but, like many people from the East End, he is worldly-wise. I was the opposite, as a youngster: I was withdrawn and shy, which didn't help my development on the pitch. He would have brought me out of my shell much quicker. That would have been of enormous benefit to me as a player.

Now Terry is manager of Barcelona, one of the biggest clubs in world football. There have been rumours that he showed interest in signing me when he first took charge of the wealthy Spanish club. But he has since signed Gary Lineker and Mark Hughes, and it seems that the chance of working with Terry has gone – although you never know what will happen in the future.

Terry Venables certainly has a sense of humour. During the time I was involved with the Under-21 squad we had a training session at Bisham Abbey in the indoor gym. Terry loves five-, six-, seven- or eight-a-side matches, and he readily joins in. On this occasion he was caught up against the wall and badly twisted his ankle, catching it between floor and wall. Poor Terry was hobbling around in a great deal of discomfort.

After training we returned to the Post House hotel, which has a massive lobby. We were grouped at one end of the lobby by the door, just passing the time, and Terry was at the bar at the far end. Billy Gilbert, who was close to Terry because of the Crystal Palace link, made a bogus telephone call. Terry Venables was paged. Billy, Vince Hilaire, Kenny Sansom and I were biting our lips as Terry came hobbling out of the bar to take his 'telephone call'. 'Did you hear that?' Billy said to Terry as he hobbled past, 'There's a call for you.' Terry struggled to the phone, which must have been 100 painful yards away. As Terry got nearer the telephone our laughter increased. We were falling about in stitches by the time he reached it. He didn't even look at us as he made his way back, but as he passed by he muttered 'I'll get you bastards on the training pitch'.

After that Terry Venables got himself a new nickname – The Man from Ankle!

Ron Greenwood

I played one and a half games in the 1982 World Cup finals under Ron Greenwood. All the time he was England manager I seemed to be used in 'bits and pieces': one game here, one game there. There was no real run of matches – two on the trot was a major sequence of games for me at that time.

It was my one big regret that Ron never threw caution to the wind to give me the run in the team that I thought I deserved. It still staggers me that he didn't play me after my debut against Bulgaria. Had he done that, I'm convinced I would have justified my place. Not only that, but my entire international career might have been completely different as a result. No doubt Ron had his reasons, but he never told me why he left me out for five games.

All right, I was only 21 and that's quite young in international terms, but I was annoyed, and more than that I was deeply hurt. But there was not very much I could do about it. I am only sorry that it eventually took so long for my international career to get properly off the ground, and that that came after Ron Greenwood's departure.

Although Ron didn't select me as often as I would have liked or as often as I thought he should have, I must say that I didn't dislike him personally, in fact I think he's a lovely fellow. He has an astute football brain, as good as any I've ever come across in the game; he can relax players, make them feel at ease, and he treats them as adults. He has quite a 'humble' approach to management: it doesn't come easy to him to 'bollock' players. It doesn't seem natural for him to be angry, he's far more at home praising people.

I have never seen Ron involved in any flare-ups with his players, it just isn't his style. He would prefer intelligent discussions in the dressing-room at half-time to disagreements or rows any day.

Remarkably, Ron Greenwood looks very much like the Football Association's administrator, Alan O'Dell. Often they were mistaken for one another as they travelled all over the world with the England party. On one trip, Ron got into the swing of the mix-up and took over Alan's job of handing out the tickets. We all thought he was going to let Alan pick the team! On another occasion, when asked for his autograph, Ron signed 'Alan O'Dell'.

Imported Players

Osvaldo Ardiles and Ricky Villa opened the floodgates for imported players after the 1978 World Cup finals in Argentina. Many have followed them, but few have made as big an impact. Ossie and Ricky achieved for Tottenham what Arnold Muhren and Frans Thyssen had done for Ipswich. They were the best of the foreign players by far.

The main advantage they had was that they were able to play for clubs that believed in good football. They were given time to settle in, and they won honours in England. Ossie's dream came true when Spurs won the FA Cup at Wembley in a match that saw Ricky score a wonder-goal which will be remembered as one of the finest individual goals in any Cup final in Britain.

From the moment Ossie came to England, the little Argentinian and I struck up an understanding on the football field. The way we hit it off straight away was almost uncanny. We have always been on the same wavelength, even in training. I have played the most enjoyable football of my career in the same team as Ossie and Ricky. The side that also fielded Steve Archibald and Garth Crooks in attack gave me the most pleasure to play in.

Any foreign player coming to Britain and succeeding has my admiration. It is easy to see why so many have failed miserably. Let's get one thing straight: the First Division is the hardest league in the world. It may not be the best technically, but it is a game of endurance, and the mental and physical demands are enormous. We play in a style that doesn't suit the Continentals. The long-ball game makes it that much harder for any foreign player to adjust. Nowhere else in the world do they play football like we do here. Alex Sabella was an Argentinian who should have made an enormous impact in England. I thought he was a superb player, but he found it very difficult to fit into the system.

For me Ossie Ardiles has been by far the most outstanding of all the imported stars. Arnold Muhren would be my second choice, with Ricky Villa third. Ricky, on his day, was the best footballer in the world. When he scored that amazing Wembley goal, he was in the middle of a purple patch that made it a pleasure to play with him. Frans Thyssen would be next on my list. Jan Molby has been a huge success, but playing for a club like Liverpool has given him a major advantage. Kasimir Denya, captain of Poland and a World Cup star, was a superbly skilful player. He never really settled in, but he was still good enough to come fifth in the rankings.

I have not been impressed by the rest of the imported players, particularly not by the strikers – not that many of the players brought over from abroad have been front men. The only foreign striker who caught my attention was the Yugoslav, Bosco Jancovic, at Middlesbrough. He impressed me when we played against them with his trickery and skill.

I was a little surprised that Spurs chose to sign Belgian World Cup striker Nico Claesen from Standard Liege for £600,000. Most of the success stories have involved midfield players, and no foreign striker has been a big hit in English football. I hope Nico settles down well, but he's in a very difficult position and he will need time. He will certainly be judged on the number of goals he scores.

4
Forward Views

Football needs a Superleague and it needs it right now. In a sense we already have a Superleague. The top clubs have the stadia, the crowd potential, the wealth; and the pulling power to attract the best players. But they also have an over-congested fixture list, with too many meaningless fixtures, too many midweek league games: in short too much football.

The fans have lost interest, and now they select their matches. They won't go to watch the mundane games against the likes of Coventry, Wimbledon, Charlton, Oxford or even Norwich. To get them out of their houses the top teams have to be on show. The game is crying out for more excellence, more big games and fewer humdrum matches of little consequence. The game is competing with so many alternative attractions. We're in the computer age, and kids of today can have all the entertainment they want in their own homes – in absolute safety. Football needs to be more of an occasion, and a family occasion at that.

I would like to see a Superleague of 18 clubs, including the four top teams from Scotland: Celtic, Rangers, Aberdeen and Dundee United. There would be sell-outs at every game. Even a match between the bottom club and the top club would be a 'big match', a good game at the highest level. My 14 top clubs from the English First Division to make up the Superleague would be: Manchester United, Liverpool, Everton, Arsenal, Tottenham Hotspur, Nottingham Forest, West Ham United, Aston Villa, Sheffield Wednesday, Newcastle, Southampton, Chelsea, Manchester City and Watford.

Tradition dies hard in football, but I believe that our national sport has reached crisis point. The game is at a crossroads. If our administrators wait for five or six years before they introduce radical change, it will be too late. Now is the time for action – not words, hesitancy and doubts.

Leisure has become a thriving industry in this country. And, with leisure activities including football becoming more and more expensive, I don't blame the public if they want to pick and chose. If I want to go to the theatre in London I have a wide choice. There are some terrific musicals around such as *Starlight Express*, *Time*, *Cats*, and so on. I know I shall be going to see a quality performance. The shows are reviewed and I know exactly what I'm going to get for my money. Not so with football: it's hit and miss. You might get a good game, if you're lucky, but the chances are you will come away dissatisfied. Even in a Superleague, obviously there are still going to be poor games, but I am sure they would be few and far between. The extra spice of the Scottish teams would ensure a cracking match, a special atmosphere and a meaningful game.

At the slightest sign of the format becoming stale, change it. Give the fans what they want: plenty of excitement; entertaining football; and matches that have value in terms of points. I know our chairman at Tottenham, Irving Scholar, has been instrumental in pushing for change. A number of top clubs threatened to break away if they didn't get their wish for a smaller First Division, a British Cup and a move toward more 'events' in the game. It took almost a year of threats, posturings, meetings, and finally a delicately negotiated package of alterations to reduce the First Division to 20 clubs over a period of two years.

No sooner has the first season of a new system started than some chairmen are doubting the wisdom of change: They don't like the idea of play-offs; the Scottish clubs are opposed to a British Cup starting just yet and our own FA probably wouldn't sanction it anyway. There are even proposals to revert back to where everything started. Crazy!

Instead of going backwards, the game should be going forward. A 20-club First Division doesn't go far enough in my view, but at least it's a start. I will be happy so long as phase two isn't too far behind it.

The country moans when the England team doesn't perform well, but if we played fewer matches and had more time to prepare for games I'm sure Bobby Robson would extract better results from his players. The England manager has campaigned vigorously on this issue. No one takes too much notice, but he's absolutely right.

I know there isn't a great deal of love lost between the Football Association and the League, but for the sake of the League game there has to be a rationalisation of the leagues. It is vital that a Premier Division of 18, perhaps even 16, should be a priority. The prospect of Celtic playing at Tottenham, of Manchester United at Ibrox, of Everton entertaining Aberdeen would ensure gates of 30,000 at every match.

I don't want to see the end of 'little' teams like Wimbledon coming through the ranks. I would want to retain the 'dream' factor by keeping promotion and relegation. But any team moving into the Premier Division would have to have their ground vetted, and if it was not up to scratch they would have to modernise their stadium to a certain standard or they wouldn't be permitted to join the Superleague.

Opponents of any Superleague scheme always point to the Third and Fourth Division clubs and argue that this would be another nail in their coffin. But I don't think a Superleague would make any difference to the lower divisions. I don't see how it would affect them at all. They are getting 1,000 people through the turnstiles now, and that wouldn't change, Superleague or no Superleague. I believe the Third and Fourth Divisions should be split into Northern and Southern Leagues, and a play-off system ought to be devised to maintain the interest as these clubs progress upwards through the divisions. Relegation and promotion should be cut to two teams instead of three, play-offs determining the final issue.

Another benefit of having an 18- or 16-club Premier League would be the likelihood of a mid-winter break. Christmas is a very expensive time, and the weather is usually so awful that games are frequently postponed anyway. Clubs object to a mid-winter break because they are worried that it would affect their cash flow. But I don't think this would be too deep a concern for the very big clubs in the Superleague.

I'm sure that bigger crowds would stimulate better performances from the players. A pop musician, for example, rehearses his routine in front of 8,000 empty seats, but when they are filled and the atmosphere builds up his performance is that much better. It's the same for any type of performer, football players included.

I would do everything possible, explore every avenue, to make the game more attractive to the fans. Millions of people are being lost to the sport every year. The game is on the decline, and not all the reasons for plummeting attendances can be laid at the door of hooliganism. The sport needs brightening up. The emphasis has to be on attacking football. Managers, coaches and players have to be given the right incentives.

I would advocate three points for an away win and two points for a home win. I am not keen on a points-for-goals system. But I would like to see a greater reward for a team winning away from home, thereby opening up games even more. Why can't the Football League and the Football Association join forces to push for rule changes which will improve the game for everyone?

One aspect of the game that annoys me as a player – and I'm sure the fans must find it pretty frustrating, too – is encrouchment at free kicks. It wouldn't even be necessary for a rule change to be passed through FIFA to correct the fault. All that is required is a strict interpretation of the existing rules. I would like to see soccer follow the example of rugby in allowing referees to punish offending players by pushing the free kick a further ten yards on. Then a player having given away a free kick 15 yards outside his penalty area is hardly going to lay himself open to penalisation for encrouchment, dissent or anything else that might jeopardise his team's chances. The threat of that free kick being moved on a further ten yards would keep everyone in check and keep the game flowing smoothly.

Another situation in which football can learn from rugby is the use of the advantage rule. It seems so much more logical in rugby – I like the idea of the referee playing the advantage just for a few seconds, long enough to know whether the side offended against has any real advantage, and if not, bringing the attacking team back and awarding a free kick. In football the referee will sometimes play advantage, but if the attacking side fails to gain any real advantage it is their tough luck. The referee makes a split-second decision on whether to play advantage, when he should be able to give himself more time to reflect on whether any real advantage has been gained.

I would also like to see a serious review of the offside law, especially when teams can catch forwards offside from a goal clearance.

Every effort must be made to discover why the fans are losing interest in football. One reason put forward is that football has always been a working man's game, and that the average working-class man is no longer able to identify with or maintain contact with the average footballer. Quite simply, some people believe certain players are vastly overpaid. But the answer to this contention is equally simple: sport has become a business. Compared to players in other major sports, footballers are badly paid. Just think of the top exponents of snooker, darts, golf, racing, motor racing and tennis – footballers are the poor relations.

Sometimes I find the attitude of the public towards footballers hard to believe. Some people are convinced that we earn what I would call 'stupid' money, fortunes. That just is not the case. I'm sure the fans believe we can pocket something like £1,000 bonus for a win. I wish we did! The only time anyone gets an accurate idea of how much the top players earn is when a club publishes its balance sheet. The reality is that precious few players come anywhere near the £100,000-a-year mark. Yet in World Championship snooker the top players are competing for prizes of £100,000 for one tournament. In the States, the sportsmen proudly boast their annual wages and winnings. Here, footballers shy away from discussing their salaries. The difference between attitudes here and in America is staggering. The American public respond to the big wage-earner. They admire him. Here, there is jealousy and envy.

There are some people in life who are completely mercenary. They want to take as much money as they can and run. Their main object is to earn as much money as possible for the least amount of work. I've no doubt that there are some footballers among them. But in sport there has to be a pride in performance. Footballers, by and large, are working-class people from working-class backgrounds. They might end up living in the stockbroker belt, but they never forget their humble beginnings. In soccer there is supply and demand. It is not a player's fault that he might be transferred for £1 million. Managers quite happily buy and sell at that inflated price. If the money was around now they would merrily continue their £1 million-a-time spending sprees.

Who can blame a player valued at £1 million or more in the transfer market for seeking a wage that reflects that value? A club's attitude is to try to fob the player off with £300 a week, and some of them might try to take advantage of a young immature lad. Little wonder that a host of professional advisers, accountants, solicitors and agents are needed in big-money transfers these days. While the clubs try to keep the wages down, the public believe that any player going for a £1 million transfer must be earning £4,000 a week, plus huge bonuses and a £100,000 signing-on fee. I can assure you that players are not earning the sort of money the public think they are.

At the very top in football there are no more than a

handful of big money-earners, no more. The vast majority of professional footballers in the lower divisions are lucky if they earn the national average wage. But if they are paid a lot less than the players at the very top that doesn't mean they do their job with any less effort or application, or indeed pride.

My attitude is simple. I feel privileged to be pursuing the sport I love as a professional. But I also have a family to support. My earning power is restricted, like that of all players, to a limited time-span. It might be ten years, it might be 15, it might be only a few years: the game is so unpredictable. A player might move to a big club abroad and hit the financial jackpot; on the other hand, injury may cut short a promising career.

The risks are high. At any time you could break a leg and go out of the game. But even a player who has a prolonged career and earns a great deal can find himself out on his ear at the age of 36 without any qualifications for other work. He virtually has to start a new life. I am not moaning, and I am not making out a case for players who are down on their luck. I'm simply arguing that footballers shouldn't be ashamed of their capacity to earn good money while they are healthy enough to enjoy it, provided they make safe provisions for the future and don't squander it.

In most sports, the 'star' performers make no secret of the fact that while they enjoy their sport, they are out to earn as much out of it as they can. In football, I'm a firm believer in freedom of contract. In any other walk of life, in any other sport, you are free to move wherever you wish once your contract has expired. Football should be no different. There is even an argument that no transfer fee should be allowed once a player is out of contract, but I feel that is going perhaps a little too far.

There can be no doubt that the biggest single factor keeping the fans away from soccer is hooliganism. Yet there is not as much trouble inside the grounds as there used to be. Better policing methods, the use of video cameras and ground improvements to enforce segregation have all helped to make stadia safer. The problems occur before and after the games, outside the grounds or at railway stations. Soccer hooliganism highlights the sickness in our society. It has to be tackled by the Government of the day – the football authorities alone cannot cope.

The biggest drawback for our game is the indefinite ban imposed by UEFA after the Heysel tragedy. Although no one can blame UEFA for not wanting our fans, the hooligan disease has now spread right across Europe, and the problems are worse in Holland, Germany and Belgium than they are in England. As a player I miss the European competition. It may not be the main reason, but it has certainly been a contributory factor in the decisions of players to leave these shores to play abroad.

Our clubs should be allowed back into Europe and one day they will be, perhaps as early as the 1987-88 season. But we shall immediately be in danger of being kicked out again. It will take only one incident involving an English club for UEFA to lose patience. Then an indefinite ban will mean 'indefinite'. It should be the responsibility of the Government to ensure that our fans do not travel abroad. They refuse to withhold passports, but they should insist on some sort of visa system for fans. There can be no doubt that UEFA will allow our clubs back only with certain guarantees concerning the travelling fans.

Another idea that should be explored further is the transmission of the away legs on giant video screens in our grounds over here. Every incentive should be given to the fans not to bother to travel. I may be in favour of curbing fans travelling abroad but I don't support a ban on fans travelling to away games in this country. We have an obligation to sort out the hooligan problem in our own backyard, but I don't see why we should be guilty of exporting it to other countries. Any away ban goes against the grain of a player. Personally, I welcome the support from our fans on our travels.

Players do get a lift from their own supporters, especially

away from home. The fans provide a better atmosphere, a climate conducive to a better game. I feel proud when our fans support us on our travels. I would not agree with Luton's method of banning all away fans. Our supporters are so much more vocal away from home. It's as if they are trying to prove they are good supporters, and most of them are. It is up to the police to root out the real troublemakers and then it's the responsibility of the courts to hammer them. I'd like to see stiffer punishments.

When you hear of cases of soccer violence when the guy gets a suspended sentence of a year or two for his third or fourth offence, it makes you feel sick, and makes the game appear inadequate in dealing with these 'crimes'. I'd like to see persistent offenders put away in prison for six months to a year minimum. Otherwise, the chances of curbing soccer violence will be greatly reduced. A hooligan let off by the courts appears in the ground the next week as an example to his mates that you can get away with acts of soccer hooliganism. I'm sure that the British Cup has been shelved because of the fear of an increase in hooliganism if Scottish supporters were frequently travelling down to English clubs.

One of the big problems is the way the media focus attention on soccer hooliganism. I detest the glorification of these idiots in the newspapers. Hooligans are interviewed, they gloat about their crimes. It only encourages others. Surely, it would be common sense for the Football League and the Football Association to call a meeting with Sports Editors and Editors of all the national newspapers to work out a combined effort to minimise the publicity given to these thugs. Naturally, any major riot has to be reported. But all the minor skirmishes should be ignored – perhaps then they might go away.

Bad language and racist remarks from the crowds are another aspect of the game that I do not like. Black players are the top targets, but I've taken as much stick as anyone over the years, especially away from home. I'm the one in the Tottenham team that the opposition fans love to hate. But I view that as a back-handed compliment. At least they recognise me! I'm baffled by the mentality of these people. If that is how they want to spend their Saturday afternoon, well, they've paid their money, it's up to them.

I've suffered some bad experiences both as a supporter and then as a player. I have always been an enthusiastic Spurs fan. I used to travel from Harlow with my mates whenever I wasn't playing myself. I once stood on the Chelsea terraces. Because we got there late for a League Cup semi-final we ended up rushing through the first turnstile we came to, and found ourselves in the notorious Shed end where all the Chelsea supporters, including some of their hard cases, massed.

One of my close school pals was Sean Fussell. He's now the manager of one of my shops. One Saturday afternoon, I went to Chelsea with Sean and his Dad. I was an associated schoolboy with Spurs at that time, so I must have been around 14 years old. We were at the front and when Spurs scored, Sean and I wanted to jump up and down to celebrate. When we realised where we were decided celebrations were not a good idea. But Sean's dad was a few steps down from us, merrily jumping up and down and yelling: 'Great goal, we've got them now!' Our heads went down as if to say 'he's got nothing to do with us, we don't even know him'. It was an embarrassing moment – a little scary, even. Fortunately nothing happened.

The worst experience of my life occurred on the terraces at Highbury. A group of ten of us went to a midweek game, which we watched from the terraces at the Clock End.

All of a sudden there was a lot of pushing and shoving. A group of Arsenal fans had sneaked up on us, manhandled us, and just as quickly they had gone. We all got on with watching the game, although I think one of our lads shouted 'Crap!' in response to their chants of 'Arsenal, Arsenal!' A couple of minutes later, one of my mates standing next to me put his hand inside his shirt because he felt something wet. When he pulled it out it was covered in blood. He had been stabbed. He didn't even realise at the time. We rushed him down to the front and he was taken off to hospital. Later we discovered that he was lucky to have survived – the blade was a quarter of an inch away from puncturing his kidney.

Then another of my mates said he felt a bit faint. We examined his head and found a huge lump. He had been hit over the head with a hammer. We had all had enough. With 20 minutes of the game remaining we left.

That episode made me feel very sour towards Arsenal although, of course, it was not the club's fault. Even so, what happened that day sickened me. It stopped me going to any more away games. I was 15 at the time and most Saturdays were taken up playing in the mornings or afternoons. I continued to watch Spurs play at White Hart Lane only. It could easily have been me stabbed that day. I was a yard away, one step down from the lad who was wounded. I can't believe all that happened simply because one Arsenal fan didn't like a Spurs supporter.

Surely that individual had a serious problem. He must have been mentally disturbed; he must have had a violent personality. If he hadn't stabbed someone at a football match he would have committed the same crime on the streets somewhere. There must have been something evil in that guy. He *wanted* to do it. No doubt he felt that he would get away with it under cover of a football match – and he did.

There's no escape from these evil types for a player, either. The secretary of the Professional Footballers' Association, Gordon Taylor, has often publicly voiced his fears that players are in grave danger from soccer hooligans, and I agree with him. Darts and an assortment of missiles are thrown from the terraces at the players, and 'fans' have even run on to the pitch to attack them. It can be dangerous taking corners or standing by the near post. It has crossed my mind that it would easy to lose an eye if a coin or dart hit you, and it could even be a lot worse than that.

Before a Charity Shield match at Wembley my head was split open by a coin hurled from the terraces. Steve Perryman was injured and I was skipper of the Spurs team playing Liverpool at the traditional curtain-raiser to the new season. As usual we had all trooped out to inspect the pitch before the kick-off. As I was walking back down the tunnel to get changed in the dressing-room, I was hit on the head by a ten pence coin thrown from a group of Liverpool fans on the terraces behind the goal.

There was a lot of blood. My suit and shirt were covered, ruined. The physio sponged me down and the doctor said I didn't need stitches. Nevertheless I was badly shaken, and the incident shocked me. I realised I was lucky to escape without serious injury. I played that day, but we lost 1–0. 'Rushie' scored, of course.

Team coaches are often a target for these people. Manchester United had a particularly unpleasant experience when they arrived at Liverpool for a game that was to be televised live when a fan squirted a substance at the players. During the 1982 World Cup finals in Spain, the England team bus was attacked. A stone was thrown, smashing a window at the front of the coach, but luckily no one was hurt.

Players have a responsibility to make sure they don't incite the crowd with any provocative gestures, but I don't accept that the players' behaviour on the field has any real influence on the conduct of the fans on the terraces. You are there to go out and play the game. You have to be aggressive to win the ball and to win the match. Some players get excited, perhaps overexcited – it depends on the individual's temperament. We have to curb our frustrations. Making V-signs to the crowd can inflame supporters. Players must be careful. Some fans, though, are out to cause trouble anyway, irrespective of what a player might or might not do.

I'm afraid that hooliganism is still a big problem that has yet to be solved. I have a 14-year-old cousin, and I wouldn't let her go to any football match on her own, so I understand how the game's supporters feel. People are scared to bring their children to football. What a tragedy for the game! New generations of soccer lovers are being lost to the sport, and those youngsters are being deprived of great entertainment. Football is still the number one sport, the most popular in the country.

I believe every club should be obliged to provide family enclosures, where parents can bring their children to watch a game in relative safety. The directors at Tottenham are certainly strongly in favour of family areas, and have started one at the club. I have to hand it to a lot of club directors. Without them many clubs would have folded by now. When the new board took over at Tottenham, Spurs were struggling financially, having committed themselves to a new £5 million stand and gigantic interest repayments. Our chairman, Irving Scholar, is a man I like and admire. I know he loves football, loves Spurs in particular and brings money into the club. There are some chairmen whose sole interest appears to be making money for themselves.

At Spurs the new board have changed the club's image. Their aim is to make the club the best in the League. They floated Tottenham Hotspur on the Stock Exchange, making it the first football club to become a public company. I bought some shares – £1,000 worth, in fact – for my little girl Zoe (actually 50 per cent of the shares are for her, the rest for me!). I didn't buy them to make a few bob, but for sentimental reasons, to make me feel as though I own a part of the club, no matter how small. I'm sure some of the other players bought them, too. Perhaps when I'm 48 and struggling to get a ticket they might let me in because I'm a shareholder!

The club has great traditions, but you cannot survive on tradition alone. Irving Scholar has pushed the club into modern times with sound promotional ideas. A football club needs to be run on business lines to prosper. He has diversified. He has set up a publishing company called Cockerel books. The first book off the conveyor belt was a club history of 25 years in Europe, and he has had the players out for signing sessions. He has also brought out a quiz book, and we all know the chairman's fetish for quizzes.

It may mean more involvement for the players, but that's

part of the changing scene. I have to agree that the club needs to get it right in the promotional sense off the field, as well as having a successful team on it. The commercialised angle has its good and bad points. I don't approve, for example, of putting up the prices for certain attractive, prestigious games – the club don't *reduce* their prices for the poorer valued games. The loyal fan who supports the club throughout the season, watching all the home games, should not be penalised when it comes to the big matches. One consolation to Spurs fans is that at White Hart Lane season ticket-holders pay no price increase for major games. The Superleague answers a lot of these questions. In my view the way to eliminate this problem is to create a climate which eliminates the unattractive games.

It is very important, from the players' point of view, to have the crowd behind the team. If you charge the fans an extra pound or more it will put their backs up. If things don't go well on the pitch they may feel more inclined to moan. In the 12 years I have played for the club I have been glad of the appreciation of the supporters for me as a player. I'm sure there are some fans who don't like me, and who never have liked me, but I sense that the majority of Spurs supporters have liked my style of play over the years.

There has always been a feeling over the time I've been at the club that it would have been far easier for the team if the crowd had been more passionate. Fans in London as a whole, and Spurs supporters in particular, seem to be more reserved than their Northern counterparts. Clubs like Liverpool, Everton and Manchester United appear to have more heartfelt support, with crowds more willing to get behind their team and create an atmosphere in the stadium. Yet on European nights there is a tremendous atmosphere at White Hart Lane, and the fans are as passionate as they are anywhere in the country. I'm sure the European nights bring out the patriotism in our supporters.

Perhaps that is the reason why, in all the club's European campaigns over the past 25 years, they have lost only once at home – ironically the last home game we played against Real Madrid, in which our skipper, Steve Perryman, unluckily conceded an own goal. We have produced tremendous European performances backed by our crowd. The supporters probably don't realise the power and influence they can provide for the players, but there is no doubt in my mind that the vocal backing has contributed to our results in Europe. The crowd can be inspirational.

England crowds at Wembley seem to lack commitment to the team and passion. It staggers me to think that certain sections of the Wembley crowd get on to the backs of the players even before the game begins. It's disturbing. I've been booed when my name has been read out before a game at Wembley. Fans from rival London clubs might be the culprits, but I don't understand their mentality. Surely, they want England to do well? They've often spent a lot of money on travel in addition to their entrance fee to support their country.

Ray Wilkins also suffered crowd abuse when he got into the England team, and several other players have gone through it. Chris Waddle is a target at the moment. You don't hear that sort of abuse at other national stadia throughout the world. The fans are partisan, they back their country – at least, they do until something goes badly wrong, and then they usually turn against them.

The Scots are passionate indeed for their team. When you go to Hampden Park, or indeed Wembley, the Celtic and Rangers fans forget their differences and back their country. But, like other nations, they do criticise their team if things go wrong, perhaps more fiercely than anyone else. But at least their first intention is to come to back their team. They've got it right there. And they desperately want their team to win.

You don't find too much passion in too many football clubs for directors. Generally, if the chairman walked to the centre of the pitch, he wouldn't get a very good reception – at least in most cases he wouldn't. Chairmen in the lower divisions may be more popular, but at the top end of the scale, they are the men the fans identify with price increases and other unpopular decisions. Sometimes a club has to make unpopular decisions. Executive boxes at Spurs are an example of how the club is catering for a minority, but an increasingly important minority.

The game has always been working-class. But facilities must improve if attendances are to be prevented from falling even lower. There are some people who simply wouldn't be interested in going to a football match if they had to suffer in the rain. If these people want executive boxes, then the club is right to provide them. I agree with these ideas to bring in money, such as Spurs Travel, the Spurs Shop and other merchandising ventures. It must be remembered, though, that the most important aspect of any football club is the team. Success on the field is the only way any club director is going to fill the stands.

I have nothing but praise for the way in which our directors handle the commercial aspect of the club. They have consulted the Prime Minister's advertising agency, Saatchi and Saatchi; they have advertised on television, they have set out to try to pull the crowds in. That can only be good for the club. I do have my doubts about selling the club's training ground at Cheshunt for £4¾ million. I am sure it makes sound financial sense to capitalise on a vast piece of real estate, which can be transformed into a profitable housing estate, but Cheshunt is the best training ground in the country. Although the dressing-room facilities might not be first-rate, there can be no better playing surface anywhere in England. Through a players eyes, this appears to be a bad step. It's a shame that a chapter in the club's history has closed. Many famous names from Spurs' glorious past have used those fields in Hertfordshire to train.

Everything changes in football, and you cannot live in the past, but when Cheshunt goes a little nostalgia, a little piece of the club's history goes with it. I suppose you have to be practical. Our chairman has a good knowledge of the game, and I'm sure we shall be found adequate training facilities, no doubt rented ones, as Arsenal have London Colney.

Synthetic surfaces are another progressive idea for the game but they are an innovation that doesn't meet with my approval. Plastic pitches make for plastic games. They are supposed to benefit the more skilful player – not in my view. The ball bounces far too high and rolls far too fast. This kind of surface lends itself to a short passing game with the ball played to 'feet', or to a long ball knocked hopefully over the defence or for a forward to win in the air.

In fact plastic pitches restrict certain skills. When I play on them there's little point in hitting my 40-yard passes. It doesn't work out that good teams necessarily play well on these pitches. In my opinion they make a mockery of the game. Although I can appreciate the financial benefits and the logic that games can go ahead when other fixtures are hit by the weather, personally, I would rather play on a mud heap than on a plastic pitch which, in reality, is no better than an icy ground.

I watched the 1987 FA Cup third round tie between Luton and Liverpool on television and to be honest I didn't enjoy it at all. The pitch is considered to be an advantage to the home team yet it messed up Luton's chances of a shock Cup win when Mick Harford was robbed of a goal as the ball bounced along the line. On a natural surface the ground would have held up the pace of the ball long enough for Harford to have scored.

I would not relish the prospect of having to play on synthetic pitches every other week, year in year out. I'm sure it would cut short a player's career. The surface might be better suited to the Continental style of football where they play with a sweeper and have a more relaxed and calculated build-up, but unfortunately it simply does not suit the rush-hour style of the English First Division.

5
The Hoddle Clan

There are ten years and three inches between my brother Carl and myself. I'm the elder and he's the taller. You could say he's 'big brother' now! But really I have always been a big brother to Carl. We have always been close. In fact, the whole family is very close.

Carl and I have played endless games in our parents' living-room. 'Cup Final' was our favourite. We would imagine we were playing at Wembley with the FA Cup at stake. Carl may have been eight at the time . . . and I was already a First Division player! There I was, kicking about with a sponge ball in the lounge or the garden during the week and then playing at Old Trafford or Anfield at the weekend, making my way in the game in my late teens.

I used to watch Carl playing on Sunday mornings for an Under-10 team. I knew he had something. He looked like me and played like me. I was sure he would have a big future in the game. I hoped he would make the grade in professional football and, more than that, I desperately wanted Carl to succeed. We were alike in many ways. Everyone commented on how he played his football with the same style, the same approach, the same look, as me. When we played together in the garden he could keep the ball up in the air for as long as I could. He had delightful touch and control even as a kid. 'I can see he's your brother', people would remark.

Even now, Carl has more 'pure' skill than anyone at Tottenham. It is one of my biggest regrets – not just in football, but in life – that Carl has not made it at Spurs the way I did. I recommended him to Spurs. I would never have mentioned him to anyone at the club unless I sincerely believed that he had a special talent and that he had a realistic chance of making the grade as a professional footballer. I had heard it all before: 'Come and look at Johnny so-and-so'. Everyone is so sure they know what it takes to make a player. They see a good young kid in the area, he may even be the best in the locality. But a big club like Spurs take the cream from Scotland, the North-East, Manchester, from everywhere in the country. You have to be more than good – you have to be a bit special.

Make no mistake, and I say it with my hand on my heart, at the age of ten Carl was head and shoulders above any other player of his age that I had seen. I know he's my brother and I'm in danger of being biased, but in fact any bias is in reverse. I know from my own experience and what I have seen of other young hopefuls that the path to success in professional football is not an easy one. I also knew that Carl would have an additional handicap – that of being my brother.

I believed in his ability – I still do – and I felt it was only fair to tell the club. Not only that, but people inside the club started to ask me about my brother, so I told them the truth as I saw it. It wasn't long before Carl was following in my footsteps. He was invited to train at the club on Tuesday and Thursday evenings after school, just as I had. He even travelled down to White Hart Lane by train from Harlow, just as I used to do.

Unfortunately for Carl, while he shared my positive traits he also possessed one of my big weaknesses. My only problem has been that I have not been blessed with electrifying pace. Similarly Carl, at the age of 15, was not naturally quick. In fact, I have to be honest and admit that he's slow, even laboured in his play. What a shame! But there is still hope for Carl. If his strength catches up with his size, I'm sure he could speed up. He could still make it. He has such vision – it would be a waste of a fine talent if he failed. Perhaps, with his height, he might develop into a footballing centre-half. Let us hope so.

There was a time when I thought he was going to make it at Spurs. He had a good season in the youth team and progressed to the reserves, whose pace he was unfortunately not up to. I'll never forget the horrible day when Carl was told he was not going to make it at Spurs. I'm not sure who was worse hit, Carl or myself. I was heartbroken. It was one of the worst days of my life.

The manager, Peter Shreeve, called me into his office. He knew I would be very emotionally affected by the club's decision. It isn't very pleasant for a kid to be told that his footballing career might be over before he has hardly had a chance. I never fully appreciated just how devastating such a verdict can be on an impressionable youngster until it happened to Carl. Peter Shreeve felt that Carl, who was just 17 at the time, had taken it pretty badly. When Peter called me into his office to break the news, I had this sick feeling in my stomach, almost as if it were happening to me.

I left Peter's office completely devastated. It's difficult to put into words exactly how broken up I felt. I was due to run round the track in a training exercise, and Carl had rushed off home. I felt choked as I ran around the track, and I quietly cried as I went around, lap after lap, thinking of nothing but Carl. The tears kept rolling down my cheeks. Perhaps I hadn't helped him enough. Perhaps I had helped him too much! I couldn't stop blaming myself. Carl had handled being my brother at school so well. It could not have been easy for him, living in my shadow. I felt he had to do it his way. I gave him all my support, watching him in the youth team before I played in the First Division on a Saturday as many times as I could. Perhaps he had been compared with me too much and that was something he was never going to beat. Perhaps I had been more of a burden to him than a help.

Had there been just a couple of years between us we might have fought and squabbled like most brothers and sisters tend to do. But with a ten-year age gap, I tended to want to look after him, want the best for him. I had been through the process of becoming a professional footballer myself. Surely with that sort of background, and his natural skills, he could make the grade? I know it must have been hard for Carl to take when his career with Spurs was cut short, but it was also hard on me. It was extremely painful for the pair of us.

Guilt was perhaps the most prominent emotion I felt that day. I could not help thinking that I should never have built up his hopes in the first place by bringing him to Spurs. I went home and the first thing I said to my Mum was: 'I feel guilty that I've made it here at Spurs and Carl has been turned away'. Later that night I poured my heart out to my wife Anne.

Well, if I was cut up and emotional, you can imagine how Carl must have felt. He was completely 'gutted', carved up. I tried to explain that he had to believe in his ability. At the same time I had to be brutally honest and explain why I felt that the club had let him go. The hard reality of soccer life was that Carl didn't have the pace – not yet. But I didn't want to be too hard on him, my main objective was to keep his spirits up.

I told him he had to go out and prove that Spurs had been wrong to release him. He wouldn't be the first player to be shown the door and then come back to make it big in professional football. I pointed to Chris Waddle and Graham Roberts. They had been turned away by clubs in their younger days, only to end up playing for England. Carl is a replica of myself. It was almost as if Spurs had thrown me out of the club.

He tried his luck at Coventry but didn't make it. He moved on to Gillingham. Funnily enough, I think he had too much ability for them, if you understand what I mean. It's a hard slog in the lower divisions. Then, through the Professional Footballers' Association, Carl got a move to a club in Malaysia. I went along with him to meet the contact who organised his stay out there. Carl went with his girlfriend, Lisa, for four months. It was good experience – even though the club folded because of bad debts! He was out there virtually on his own, away from the family ties for the first time in his life. I admired him for going. He returned a changed man. He's grown up, more mature.

Carl has now joined the 'Brothers' XI' team, Barnet. I call it the brothers' team because Kenny Sansom's brother David also plays for the non-league side together with the third of the Stein brothers. Mitchell Thomas's cousin also turns out for the club. Carl is working for a print warehouse and book distribution company, Longman, involved with computers. He tells me that he doesn't know how the company has survived all these years without him! He is now engaged to his girlfriend, Lisa. I would give anything to help Carl to resurrect his career and become a full-time top professional. I would willingly sacrifice a year of my own career to see him achieve that. I do feel very sorry for him.

The Hoddles are a very close-knit family. I love my brother, but he could have grown up hating me. He has taken a lot of stick throughout his school life for being the brother of a famous footballer. He could have envied my success, but he hasn't. If anything I believe he's proud of what I've achieved – he calls me the best footballer in the world! There's not an ounce of hatred or envy in him towards me. Carl has got into plenty of scraps over me. Even though at the age of 18 he was 6ft 4ins tall someone decided to sort him out merely because he was my brother. He was out at a rugby club with some of his friends and this bloke was looking for trouble. There was a scuffle and punches were thrown, but luckily it was stopped before it really got started.

The Hoddle name has probably been a massive handicap to carry in his growing up stage. But it can have its advantages, too, for example, it probably helped as an introduction to the club in Malaysia. The Hoddles are a Harlow clan. It's frightening just how close a family unit we are – not just emotionally, for we actually all live in Harlow.

We call our Mum Terry, but her real name is Latisia and she is also known as Teresa. My dad is Derek, or 'Del Boy' as my daughter Zoe calls him. When my parents were married Mum's name got mixed up and came out as La Tit-sia. That's been a standing joke in the family for years. Carl lives with our parents on one side of Harlow. I live with Anne, and our two lovely daughters, Zoe Anne and Zara Marie, on the other side of town. There's my uncle, Dave Hoddle, and cousins 11-year-old Mark and 14-year-old Michelle, and 73-year-old Nan Hoddle – all living in Harlow.

My uncle Dave was the original Hoddle at Tottenham. He had a spell at the club as a goalkeeper. Many people in Harlow confuse Dave with my brother Carl. They seem to think that Dave is my older brother. It's an easy mistake to make, I suppose – there's eight years between Dave and myself, and ten years between myself and Carl. When I was younger I played in the same team as my uncle and Dad. Dave was like an elder brother to me. He was a good amateur footballer for a spell, but he wasn't dedicated enough to make the grade at Spurs. He went training there for a year. But he liked a pint and thought he was Jack the Lad. He got despondent after a while and didn't bother turning up. But I've seen him play and I've been impressed. He has played for Ware, Harlow Town, and Bishops Stortford in his time.

Michelle loves her dancing, particularly ballet, and there might be another footballing Hoddle rolling off the conveyor belt in young Mark, who plays for KC Dynamoes in the Harlow District League. He's got a chance – I watched him play in one game where he scored a hat-trick, including two staggering volleys.

It's not only every Christmas that the Hoddle family get together – we meet up virtually every other Sunday. We have a swimming pool in our garden, and we enjoy lovely summer Sundays there with the whole family.

My Dad was a player with Stoke and Brentford, as well as a top-class amateur footballer with Harlow and Edgware. But he has always told me that he didn't teach me anything about the game. He says that, at the age of six or seven, I was doing things with the ball that he couldn't do at the peak of his career. Nevertheless, I'll always be grateful to my Dad, and indeed, to my Mum for their support.

As a child, I was always waiting with a football tucked under my arm for Dad to come home from work. In the Harlow Town park there are two trees perfectly placed to act as two goalposts, and we would play there until it was dark. When I was seven or eight, there was many a night when my Dad would leave me sitting under a tree crying my eyes out when he wanted to go in – because it was pitch black! Dad would return home and Mum would ask: 'Where's Glenn?' Dad would say: 'He's crying and complaining that I've come back in'. Perhaps I might have become disillusioned with the game if it hadn't been for my Mum and Dad. My Mum used to get more het up than my Dad when they watched me play in the early days.

I suppose you could say that I had an eventful childhood. My parents tell me that I had nine lives. I gave Mum her biggest shock when I was only two years old. Oddly enough it involved football. Mum was watching Dad play one bitterly cold January day. There was snow on the ground and she considered it too cold to keep me outdoors. She was able to watch the match from a friend's flat, where she sat with me in front of an open window.

Mum hadn't been able to decide earlier in the day whether to dress me in long trousers or a short pair with turn-ups. She was going to put me in the long trousers, then for some reason changed her mind. She turned round to speak to someone in the room, and suddenly, I had gone, slipped out of her grasp and out of the window. She flung out her arms and caught me by my turn-ups. The flat was high up, and I'd have been a goner if she hadn't grabbed me. My Mum cried her eyes out, but she was thankful for those turn-ups!

My next near miss came at the age of about four or five. I ran across the road without looking where I was going. I heard my Dad scream, and I froze. There was an enormous articulated lorry heading straight for me. My dad says that, to this day, he doesn't know how the lorry missed me. It passed right by my toes. Had it been my mother who had screamed, I might not have reacted the way I did, but it was unusual to hear my Dad yell. I'm convinced it was my fate to be saved. I've always felt that your destiny is written out before you.

My belief in fate is probably the main reason I don't get hurt by all the knockers gunning for me. When I look back over my life I realise that whatever happens was meant to happen.

In fact, I came perilously close to never playing football, perhaps never playing any sport. I was 15 at the time, and I had begun training regularly at Tottenham and was due to sign associated schoolboy forms for the club that Easter. I was captain of the school cricket team. Like a real 'muggins' I decided, in this particular match, to put myself close to the batsman to try to sneak a catch. There was a full toss, the batsman let fly, and the ball caught me right underneath the eye. There was no getting out of the way.

I was driven home. Already the eye had swollen badly and was black and blue. I looked like the Elephant Man. I'm sure my appearance must have shocked my Mum and Dad, but they didn't know just how badly I'd been hurt. I owe a great deal to Mr Godsman, our Headmaster. He had heard about my accident at the cricket match and he came round to see how I was. He took one look at my eye and said 'Oh my God, get him into hospital at once'.

He recommended the Harlow Hospital to check it over. The nurse put me on the bed and the doctor was sure something was wrong, so I was whisked off the Eye Hospital in Bishops Stortford. There was a haemorrhage behind the eye. There was a 50-50 chance that I would lose the sight in my right eye. I was told I had to lie without moving for a week to ten days, possibly two weeks. I had to stay perfectly still, with a patch over the bad eye, staring at the ceiling.

Naturally, it is impossible to lie in bed so still for so long. When no one was looking I would wander around, or let my eye search out the television, or turn around to listen to the radio. I remember that the Test Match was on at the time, and couldn't bear to miss any of the action.

One day, while I was still in hospital and the doctors were still worried my Mum broke down in tears. Finally, the truth came out. Unless I stared at that ceiling and hardly moved, I would lose the sight for sure. My Mum's confession did the trick, all right. I can still remember that ceiling to this day. From that moment I never took my good eye off it. I just wish the doctors had told me. No doubt they didn't want to frighten me, but for the first few days before I knew, I wasn't able to concentrate on the ceiling and I allowed my eye to wander. It was a dreadful feeling, as you can imagine, and I am lucky to have come through it. My football career could easily have been finished before it had even begun.

Over the years I have had true and magnificent support from my whole family. They have always stood by me whenever things have gone wrong. If anything, it has been harder for them than it has for me to take the knocks. They've been hurt by some of the headlines and the criticism. There have been times when my parents have sat in the stands watching me play, and Mum has felt like bashing some of the supporters with her handbag. They're naturally very proud of my achievements and my good name, but they also get annoyed if the fans unjustifiably criticise some of the other players in the team. On occasions Dad has been forced to drag Mum away. After one match at West Bromwich, they were walking away from the ground after the game when Mum spotted some hooligans staging a pitched battle across the road. Mum started to run them down, telling them what she thought of them. Dad thought it was wise to pull her away, and he was right. He was pretty annoyed, and he doesn't often lose his temper, but he realised there could have been serious trouble if the thugs had turned nasty.

My parents have always been on hand to talk about problems when I've needed them, and, as well as my family, I've also had some very good friends, particularly Eileen who guided me through perhaps the worst period of my soccer career, when I had serious doubts about whether I'd ever play again. Our relationship is recorded more fully elsewhere in this book.

I was out of the game for the best part of a year with an Achilles' injury that needed an operation. During that time, I looked at the game from a different point of view. I knew that when I got back I would make the most of my abilities – I would become an even better player. I changed my attitude and my approach to the game.

That could well prove to be the most crucial point in my footballing career. As a result of my new attitude I became harder, not in the sense that I'd go rushing around kicking opponents, but harder from within, harder as a person. Also I was no longer afraid to hurt opponents – after all I had been hurt myself. For years I had been singled out for special attention by defenders, from the legal man-to-man marking to more ruthless tactics. I had become a target: stop Hoddle and you'll stop Tottenham. Many managers had that approach, but it was nonsense, of course. I was not a one-man team, and I've never considered myself indispensable. On the contrary, my long spell out proved conclusively to me that the team can perform without me. It also made me realise that I must appreciate my own talents more.

The frustrations I suffered as a result of being side-lined so long *did* make me a better player afterwards. Now I'm no longer worried that opponents are going to come to confront Spurs with the intention of kicking lumps out of me all afternoon. Don Howe spotted this problem with me four years ago. He knew I didn't like to be man-for-man marked, and that it caused me a mental problem: if I knew I was going to face a barrage of kicks, it would stop me playing my natural game. Don always said I couldn't rely on my ability alone, and that I would have to meet force with force. I am no longer afraid to do just that. I am prepared to go into a tackle hard but fairly, and I am not concerned if I kick an opponent accidentally.

Far from viewing man-for-man marking as something that should concern me, I see it as a challenge, an obstacle to be overcome, a problem that I can master. I can now handle the physical side of the game. I've been clattered so often in the past that I think it's about time I started to dish some out. I'm paying the price for it: I'm getting booked more often. But I assure you that I never maliciously go in to hurt an opponent. Unfortunately, I cannot say the same for certain players that have tackled me. Reuben Agboola was guilty of one of the nastiest fouls of which I have ever been on the receiving end. It was early in the game when the Southampton defender kicked me on the knee – hard. I was carried off. I suppose if you keep getting kicked you tend, eventually, to want to kick back. Early in my career I was reluctant to hurt anyone, but that's all part of growing up and learning from experience.

I doubt that this toughening up process, which has come about for whatever reasons, has had a bad effect. It has probably made a better all-round player of me in the latter years of my career. It has always annoyed me that I am looked upon as some 'fancy dan' footballer because I'm a skilful player who enjoys his role as a play-maker. It is often said of me that I have an elegant style, but that I am not really a winner in the Graham Roberts mould. That is absolute nonsense, and what is more, it hurts. I want to be a winner as much as anyone, including Graham Roberts. If I played table tennis against my uncle at home I would want to beat him – I have always been like that.

Actually, tennis is the game I love. Garth Crooks, when he was at Spurs, shared my passion for the game. One hot summer we played a five-set match lasting four hours and he was furious because he failed to beat me. There was no way I was going to lose that match – we were both playing for a big prize in our eyes – our pride.

In addition to doing my job on the football field, I have a wide variety of other interests and commitments connected with the game. From mid-July to August I run a soccer coaching school for youngsters in Bournemouth. I go there once or twice a week to coach. We have a resident coach, Les

Parodi. It is a four-week residential course, and we also take in local lads. We have had as many as 700 boys over that period. It is part of a wider sports-for-all scheme, including tennis, squash and other courses. Besides taking coaching sessions on my summer courses I coach the Glenn Hoddle Sports team that plays in the Harlow League. Perhaps when I finish playing I might want to stay in the game as a coach, or maybe even move into management. Although I've enjoyed my career in football, I may on the other hand turn to other things in life that I might want to do – I'm not really looking that far ahead.

I also have a sports and leisure business in Epping, which is run by my school pal Sean Fussell. Sean is like a brother, and I spend a lot of time with him socially. We hope to move the shop to Bishops Stortford soon. Our newest business venture is a pro-am service that we are starting up in Bournemouth. If it is successful we hope to expand nationwide. The idea is to arrange for a football club everything that it might want: kit; tours in Europe; trophies; dinner-and-dances, autographed footballs or shirts. It will be ideal for Sunday League sides and schools. I started my football in the Sunday Leagues, so they are close to my heart!

For the past four years I've had a contract to write for the *Sun* newspaper, and at one time I had a column in *Match Weekly* magazine. I'm often asked to open garages, etc. I drive a Peugeot sponsored car. I have my own leisure wear range with Hummel, which I help to design. There's a Glenn Hoddle boot as well as a Glenn Hoddle football.

Friendships are very important to me and, in common with most people, I have many friends of my own age. However, one of the closest friendships I have forged is with John Gorman. I am sure that Spurs fans will remember John – he joined the club from Carlisle to replace Cyril Knowles, whose career was ended through injury. John was 29 and I was 19 at that time but in spite of the age difference we got on famously, and so did our families. Anne and I are still close to this day to John and his wife Myra, and

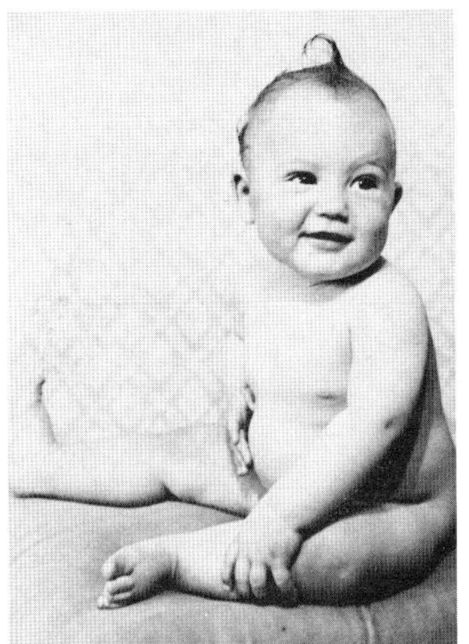

At a few months old my hairstyle left something to be desired (above left). My passion for cricket developed early (above right) although later on it almost cost me an eye. Aged 12 with the Spinney Dynamos (below). I'm the one with the ball, of course!

Carleton Photographic Se vices Limited

My wife Anne and I on our wedding day.

There's never a dull moment with Zoe Anne and Zara Marie, our two lively daughters.

Daily Mirror/Monte Fresco

Bob Thomas Sports Photography

White Hart Lane has been the scene of some marvellous European games. Feyenoord's Johann Cruyff and I compete for the ball in the UEFA Cup second round first leg match in 1983. I had a great game, creating all four goals for Tottenham.

Daily Mirror/Monte Fresco

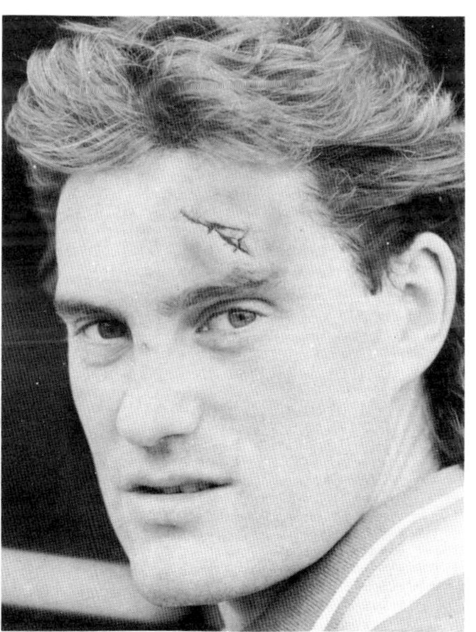

It isn't all glory, though – Jakubec Sloup of Bohemians Prague left me with a reminder of Spurs' 1984 battle in Czechoslovakia for a place in the UEFA Cup quarter-finals.

Daily Mirror/Monte Fresco

The Hoddle brothers. Unsuccessful at Spurs, happily Carl has found a niche at Barnet.

Colorsport

After my clash of heads with Steve Hodge in the 1986 International against Yugoslavia I was hailed as a hero, but the press are just as quick to slate me, too.

Roy Chaplin

With former England manager Ron Greenwood. My one big regret is that he didn't select me more often.

Daily Mirror/Monte Fresco

Peter Shreeve, first coach then manager at Tottenham, makes a point. He gave me some sound advice that helped me at a crucial stage of my career.

Bob Thomas Sports Photography

Eddie Keogh

Poland's Wlodimiercz Smolarek challenges me (above), but England emerge 3–0 victors in our first win of the World Cup finals. Diego Maradona (below), perpetrator of the notorious 'handball goal' in our match against Argentina, with Hoddle in pursuit.

Bob Thomas Sports Photography

Press Association

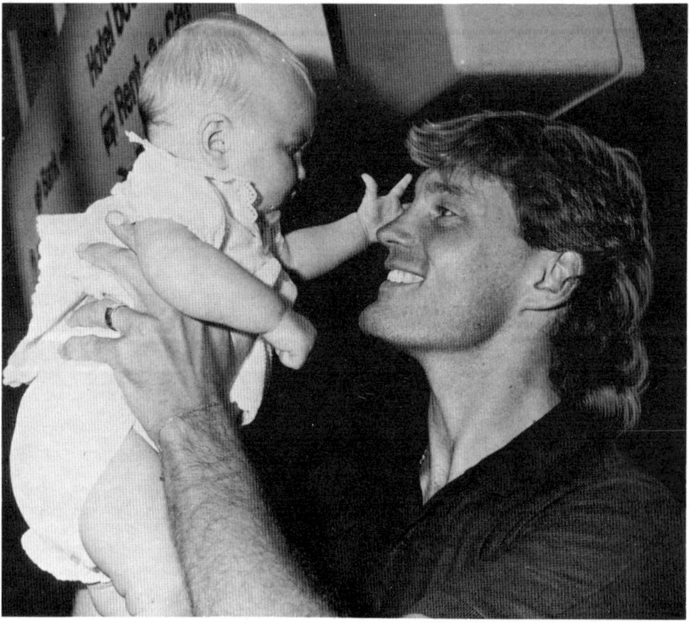

England's World Cup hopes are dashed after losing 2–1 to Argentina. Manager Bobby Robson offers a word or two of solace but the circumstances of our defeat were a bitter blow. Back at Heathrow baby Zara offers a tentative greeting. I didn't even recognise her when she was handed to me!

he is godfather to our daughter Zara. He is now coach to Gillingham's youth team and lives near us at Cheshunt.

When John was forced to quit League football through injury he went to the USA where he was in fact able to resume his career as a player. He invited Ossie Ardiles and me out there to play as guests for his club, Tampa Bay Rowdies. It was a great experience and I enjoyed playing again with John. There was a crowd of 35,000 and a really splendid atmosphere, with a firework display and all the facilities you could want for a great family day out. I am sure there is something to be learned by football in Britain from the way the Americans put on an event. That was a thoroughly happy two weeks' holiday for my family and after guesting for Tampa Bay I moved on to Canada to play for a European eleven.

I lead a very busy life but I try to make time to visit a children's hospice as often as I can, as well as other hospitals. I want to get more involved in helping children. I have two lovely children of my own and I thank God that they are healthy. We all take so much for granted. I like to spend as much time with my own children as I am able, but I also like to help others.

6
The Tottenham Way

Bill Nicholson

It is impossible for me to sit in judgement on Bill Nicholson – I was only 16 in Bill's last season in management. But Nicholson's 16-year reign as Tottenham manager hardly needs an assessment. He was simply the best, and his record speaks for itself.

When I first arrived at the club, he commanded such respect that we were all in awe of the great man. If we saw him coming along the corridor we'd rush out of his way. He was like the Headmaster at school. He would come along to watch the youth team in the morning when I was playing. Whenever he turned up it was a huge incentive to do well and impress him. I heard a story that Bill was tempted to throw me into the first team at the beginning of his final season when things were not going too well. Obviously, he decided against it, but I'm not sure how true it was that he considered giving me my big chance then.

In my view Bill Nicholson *is* Tottenham Hotspur. The success he has brought the club is phenomenal. Bill Nicholson is on a par with the truly great managers of his time like Bill Shankly and Sir Matt Busby: they are all legends. Because of that it must be difficult for any manager to step into their shoes. It has certainly been a problem at Manchester United and Spurs, although they seem to have overcome the obstacles at Liverpool. Although we don't see so much of Bill these days, he is still very much a part of the club, scouting future transfer targets and keeping an eye on the opposition.

Terry Neill

Terry Neill was a total outsider. Having no Tottenham connections, he was an odd appointment for the club. It has been said that the late Sidney Wale did not realise that his choice of manager to succeed Bill Nicholson was a former Arsenal player. I find that hard to believe! It was always going to be difficult for a former Arsenal player to be accepted as a Spurs manager, especially the man replacing a legend like Bill Nicholson. To cap it all, this was Neill's first big managerial post, coming as he did from Hull City and as part-time boss of the Northern Ireland team.

In some respects I owe Terry Neill a lot. After all it was Neill who handed me my First Division debut when I was not quite 18. But we had our differences. It seemed to me that he picked on the young players like myself, making examples of us to highlight his authority. A certain amount of resentment built up and came to a head during an end of season tour in Australia. For some reason Terry got on to the backs of Steve Walford and myself. The frustrations grew as everything that went wrong turned out to be the fault of Steve or myself, or the pair of us. In training, we were the players to be singled out. I don't mind criticism if it is valid, but in most cases on that tour it wasn't. At that stage of my development such treatment did not help. I revolted.

I wasn't very keen on Neill's view of the game. In my opinion he lacked ideas as a coach, and wasn't the best at man-management, either. It was hard for me to see what his qualities actually were as a manager or a coach. I didn't really agree with a lot of the points he tried to put over. I listened more to Keith Burkinshaw than I did to Terry Neill and his thoughts on football. It was clear to me that Neill brought in Keith Burkinshaw as his coach because he was not getting through to the players himself.

I looked forward to learning when I came into the first team, I expected that my soccer education would really take off, but I learned more from one session with Terry Venables with the England Under-21s than I ever did in two years with Terry Neill.

When I returned from that tour of Australia and I told my Mum and Dad that I didn't feel like staying at the club the next season. I was depressed enough to leave when I saw a news bulletin on television that said that Terry Neill had resigned. I did not feel at all upset by that news.

Keith Burkinshaw

Although Terry Neill gave me my big chance in the Tottenham first team it was under Keith Burkinshaw that I played my first full season, and what a start it was! We suffered relegation in Keith's first season as manager, but the board showed enormous courage by sticking with him. Their loyalty was amply rewarded in my view. We won promotion at the first attempt and went on to win two FA Cups in successive seasons, and in Keith's eighth and final year we won the UEFA Cup.

The players were determined to win the UEFA Cup, as much for the manager as for ourselves. Keith was a good manager, he was honest with his players – sometimes too honest. He didn't beat about the bush, he told us exactly what he thought of us. But Tottenham's enormous success under Keith was not brought about solely by his good management. His coach, Peter Shreeve, had been elevated to the first team about the time that our success began to gain ground. That was no coincidence. Pat Welton was Keith's original first team coach, but Pat's vocation was with the reserve and youth team players. He was one of the best coaches I have ever come across. Unfortunately he didn't have the respect of the senior players brought in from other clubs, which became a problem for Keith. He solved it by promoting Peter Shreeve. A large percentage of Tottenham's achievements at this time can be attributed to Peter Shreeve's work.

There was a great deal that was clear-cut about Keith Burkinshaw. He always promoted his image as a Tottenham man, often stating publicly that the Spurs philosophy was also his. His purchase of Ossie Ardiles and Ricky Villa was an example of how he like to carry on the Tottenham traditions of open, attacking, neat-passing football. The truth was that he was lucky with his signings of the two Argentinian World Cup players. He was never really convinced that he ought to buy them, and the deal was actually first mooted by Terry Neill at Arsenal.

In reality, I believe that deep down Keith would have preferred a long-ball game. I'm sure he would have liked a battling style. He was always having a go at me about my work rate and my commitment to the team. Fair enough, he was entitled to do that, and I agree that every player has to do his share of the work. But nothing was ever shades of grey with Keith, it had to be black or white. All players are different: some need gentle handling, others need a kick up the backside; some players are better creating than they are destroying.

Keith always insisted that I did more defending. I was given the impression that he would have been happier if I had done more defending than attacking. Now, that wasn't how I saw it at all. Keith wanted me to attack and defend equally, while I felt I should divide my time 70–30 in favour of offensive play. At that time he shoved down my throat his feelings that I shirked my defensive duties. That's where he and I disagreed. Of course, I'm fully aware of my defensive deficiencies. But I do have the ability to open up opponents' defences and be creative. That, in my opinion, is more important: it is positive play, not negative. There are not too many creative players around, and there are far too many destructive players – that, in my opinion is what is wrong with English football.

I know where my strengths lie, and I was determined to stick by my principles. It wasn't easy at times, especially as at that stage of my career I was getting a lot of criticism from outside the club. The big debate was underway, with a lot of people putting in their tuppenceworth about whether I was good or bad for English football. Football should be a blend of strengths and styles – it is a team game. At that time I didn't possess the strength to attack and defend for a full 90 minutes. We had players in the side like Steve Perryman, John Pratt and Ralph Coates who could do all the running around you could ask of them. I did my percentage of defensive work, but I needed more freedom to express my skills and create goal-scoring chances.

It was bad enough suffering the doubters from without, but when they materialised from within – in the person of my own manager – it was even harder to take. Perhaps I should have taken issue with him over this. I never did, but it hung over my head, and I'm sure the public began to believe that I hardly bothered to try after the comments from our manager. However, I never allowed it to get me down because I had plenty of faith in my own ability to survive.

The best answer I have for my critics, and that obviously includes Keith Burkinshaw, is that a player with less ability than myself would not be chased by the manager to create more goals and goal chances than he is capable of. Yet players with the ability to create goal chances are told to increase their work rate. That problem encapsulates exactly what is wrong with English football. Too much emphasis is placed on work rate, on runners, and not enough on skill and the freedom to express it. The English First Division is a hard arena for skilful, attacking midfield players, and a lot of skill is knocked out of players at an early age. Demands for more of the Seb Coes of football, perhaps more than anything else, have put the English game back in terms of world status. I was strong-willed enough to resist the pressures on me to concentrate on defending rather than attacking, so it was obvious that one day Keith Burkinshaw and I would clash. It finally happened at Christmastime in 1978. I wasn't playing particularly well, and I was dropped. Looking back, I would concede that perhaps I deserved to be left out, in view of my form at the time. After the match, at Queens Park Rangers, when we returned to our ground, I stepped off the coach determined to have it out with the manager.

I had boiled over, and that's rare for me – it is alien to my temperament. I felt that if the manager wanted four workmanlike players in his midfield then there was no future for me at the club. I was really upset and my emotions were running high. I asked for a transfer. I'd had enough. I wanted my transfer request to become public knowledge because I was ready for other clubs to move in for me. This was the only time in my life that I envisaged leaving Spurs for another club in this country.

I rang a journalist friend of mine who naturally ran the story. To illustrate Keith's paranoia with the Press, he accused the journalist of having instigated the story, and banned him from the club. In retaliation, Keith publicly hit back saying I was acting like a spoilt child.

Looking back, we both acted like children. It was such a silly row, and I was foolish to have asked for a move. Keith asked me to put it in writing. I never did, and within two weeks I was back in the team, the whole episode forgotten.

Keith Burkinshaw's style of management worked well enough for him. But sometimes I wonder how he managed it – he made some big mistakes, and man-management was not his strong point. One of his greatest mistakes was his handling of Steve Archibald. Granted, there was an incident between the two. Archibald thought he was badly injured in our home match against Coventry. He wanted to come off late in the game, fearing he would do more damage. But we were already down to ten men and the manager asked 'Archy' to carry on – even hobbling he would be of nuisance value. Archibald refused and left the field, but the very next day he turned up for training . . . and trained!

The manager blew his top, quite rightly. But his big error of judgement was to make the row public, slamming Archy in the newspapers.

There can be no doubt that their squabble affected team spirit. Archy's attitude towards his team-mates changed in the context of the game. He became selfish in his desire to prove the manager wrong. The irony is that Burkinshaw came out a winner – Archibald did prove him wrong, but playing so well for himself and scoring so many goals partly backfired on him by covering Keith in reflected glory. Indirectly Burkinshaw had motivated a lethal scoring force. Eventually Barcelona snapped up Archibald for £1,150,000 with Spurs being paid in dollars and making a little extra on the exchange rates.

I believe the team as a whole suffered as a result of the Archibald affair. I loved to play with Archy and Garth Crooks. They were ideal for me, and I was perfect for them. In the end I could 'find' Archy and Garth with my eyes shut. They knew all they had to do was to make a run forward into space and I would drop the ball into their stride. It was a perfect relationship, the ideal understanding. At times it was almost telepathic.

In my view Archy was an exceptional player. He had the skill, the touch, and the will to win. At first I thoroughly enjoyed playing with him and Garth. Then Archy changed. You could see it in his game. He was playing for himself, not the team, after his bust-up with the manager. Garth and Archy had always had a healthy competition for goals, each of them wanting to be top scorer, but had always helped each other, laying on scoring chances for each other until Archy went into his mood. That was such a great shame for everyone. One of his great strengths, apart from goal-scoring, was making decoy runs for other players, a skill we badly missed.

At this time Mark Falco was given an increasing number of games and he deserved a medal every time he played with Archy. Our Scottish international top striker would not make himself available for any chasing back or closing down defenders. He stayed in a central position waiting for a break, just poaching for goals. Poor Mark was sprinting 69 or 70 yards at a time to make space up front. Not only was he doing his own running about, he was doing all Archy's donkey work as well.

Archy totally rebelled against the management. He was

not interested in Keith Burkinshaw, nor in anything that he had to say. He was no longer interested in the club and no longer loyal to the team. He caused a great deal of resentment in the dressing-room. Sure, he still scored a lot of goals, but there were many times when he could have created chances for others and he chose not to. He had become selfish and arrogant. His behaviour caused a split in the camp. Many of the players thought he was wrong, and not just in his attitude to the manager after their confrontation. His insistence on leaving the field in the incident that sparked off the row was not a popular move. The majority at Spurs felt that Archy should have played on against Coventry for the good of the team and for the sake of his team-mates. I think some of the players would not forgive him for that decision alone.

Steve Archibald was not the 'loner' everyone thought he was. At least, that was the case when he first joined the club from Aberdeen for £850,000. He became extremely friendly with quite a few of the players, especially Ossie Ardiles, Chris Hughton and Garth Crooks. Ossie is still very close to Archy and has kept in touch with him during his career under Terry Venables at the Nou Camp in Barcelona. But there were a few players, and I include myself in this category, who felt he was too wrapped up with himself on the pitch, particularly after the rumpus with the manager.

Despite what I have said about Steve Archibald, I still maintain he was a fine player, and a far better player before his row with the manager.

Keith Burkinshaw clashed with another Scotsman, not long after Archibald left Spurs for Spain. This time it was Alan Brazil, who joined us from Ipswich Town for a £450,000 fee and was very quickly sold on to Manchester United. Surprisingly, even though Brazil was unsuccessful at Spurs, the club still managed to make a tidy profit on the transfer, Manchester United paying £750,000 for him. Alan just did not seem to be a big city player. He didn't quite make it at Spurs, although he started well, his goals contributing to our push towards European qualification. He also failed at Old

Trafford, and soon he was on his way back to London, via a spell with Coventry, to join Queens Park Rangers.

The clash between Alan and Keith was simply a question of personalities. The manager dropped Alan from the team and expected him to react by playing well in the reserves to try to justify a recall. Not Alan – his attitude was that if he scored a hat-trick or even five goals in a reserve game it would be nothing to get excited about. He was a first team player and he wasn't prepared to put himself out in the reserves. Keith, by contrast, demanded that he ran around and showed a bit of interest. It was inevitable that this vast gulf between their viewpoints would cause friction.

Their differences came to a head when the manager bombed Alan out of the UEFA Cup squad. Alan's goals had got the club into Europe, but the manager had had enough of him. It was clear that Alan would have to leave the club. Alan is very laid-back in his ways, but he's a smashing lad. Keith just couldn't get on with him professionally. Alan needed someone to inspire him; he needed motivation from the manager, but what he got was confrontation. He suffered one knock after another, and he was continually frustrated by injuries and lack of form. Peter Shreeve is the type of character who would have brought the best out of Alan. If he had been manager at the time he would have done a lot for Alan's confidence. It was a ridiculous situation because, deep down, Keith actually quite liked Alan, and Alan didn't dislike Keith.

Keith Burkinshaw's problem was that he treated all his players the same, not accounting for the fact that sometimes a player needs a little coaxing, a little affection, some understanding. Alan Brazil was one of those players. In spite of their mutual respect, Keith and Alan did not seem able to forge any kind of relationship. That can only be seen as bad man-management on Keith's part.

Despite some faults, Keith was a huge success at Spurs. He won the UEFA Cup as a defiant farewell gesture to the board that had decided he was no longer good enough for the club. Perhaps they felt that eight years in one place was long enough. Perhaps they felt that Keith was unable to adapt to the modern game.

Spurs by this time had become a publicly quoted company on the Stock Exchange. Keith had complained about being answerable to the shareholders as well as to the fans and the board. He believed that the manager should be the focal point of the club and that everything should revolve around him. He wanted to deal with transfer negotiations and players' contracts himself while the board wanted more control over the finances. At least that is how it appeared, although, as a player, I don't know exactly why Keith left the club.

In my view, it is an indication of the sad state of football when a manager resigns after winning a major European trophy. That doesn't make much sense to me. Everyone at the club wants success: the players, the manager, the board and the supporters. Keith Burkinshaw brought them that success. What more could he have done? I suppose the board wanted even greater prizes, such as the League Championship. Perhaps Keith Burkinshaw simply was not the type of manager the new Tottenham board wanted. But it seems staggering that a manager can be allowed to leave after bringing home the UEFA Cup. Even now the real reason for Keith's departure remains a mystery. Perhaps there was a part of him that was happy to leave on a high note – that I wouldn't know about.

Keith Burkinshaw turned his back on English football for a reason I do not know. No doubt he earned a fortune as national team manager in Bahrain for two years. Perhaps he was not prepared to switch to another club only to find that another chairman really wanted a glorified coach as opposed to a manager. It was not all one-way traffic – it must not be forgotten that he did well out of Spurs. He was granted a testimonial, and was given a golden handshake. The whole episode baffled not only me, but also the rest of the players. Some of them had had their ups and downs with Keith, but I'm sure we were all sorry to see him go.

Peter Shreeve

Keith Burkinshaw was replaced by Peter Shreeve, who had been a long time at the club and had been in charge of the youth team when I first joined. I always enjoyed his training methods. Training can be a chore, but Peter made the sessions interesting. He had plenty of good ideas, placing the emphasis on skill and improvement of touch and control. I'm convinced he made us into better players.

In my opinion he made the transition from coach to manager successfully. The critics who said he was an excellent coach but a poor manager got it wrong – for the most part they were people who knew nothing about it. The only difference between coach and manager is that the manager takes the responsibility of backing his judgement in the transfer market, and I don't think Peter made any errors in his buying and selling. Peter Shreeve has a lot to offer football, and I was shocked when he was sacked by Spurs after just two years in charge of team affairs.

Some managers don't bother to turn up for training, but Peter was always there, working with his players. He had had much to do with the success of his predecessor Keith Burkinshaw. During Peter's time as coach we won two successive FA Cups as well as the UEFA Cup.

Fifty per cent of the work behind that success story and the credit for the motivation of the players was attributable to Peter Shreeve. He worked very closely with us, and we respected him. The players responded positively to him because they believed in his coaching techniques. He was accused of not doing enough when he was finally elevated to the status of manager. Hang on a minute! He didn't do so badly when he was coach, and I feel that contribution was overlooked when the decision was made to dispense with his services.

When I think back to Keith Burkinshaw's reign, it seems as though Peter Shreeve's career followed a similar path. Burkinshaw was upgraded from first team coach to manager and in his first season took the team down from the First Division to the Second. The big difference was that the board, at that time, decided to give Keith a chance. Their patience was rewarded when we were promoted the next season. I don't think the current board were prepared to be as tolerant with Peter Shreeve.

Surely two years in management is not time enough to make a reliable assessment? The decision to stick by Keith worked out, so why wasn't Peter given a longer period to establish himself? I feel sorry for Peter. I believe he was unfortunate to lose his job. In fact, he made a bright start to his first season, and we nearly won the Championship. The argument has always been that, for the past quarter of a century, Spurs have rarely, if at all, challenged for the League title since winning it in 1961. Only a serious injury to Gary Stevens put the skids under our title challenge that year, and it started to go wrong in the latter part of the season.

I agree that the second season under Peter Shreeve was a flop. But he didn't make many changes to the personnel or to the system that had nearly carried off the title the season before. I have to take my share of the responsibility for that along with the rest of the players. We let Peter down, it's as simple as that. A number of people hit bad form and lost confidence. It was a bad season, and it came at a time when the board were seeking success. Perhaps they were a touch spoiled by the excitement of having come so close the previous season.

The chairman, Irving Scholar, had given Peter Shreeve a new improved contract at the start of the season, extending it by a further year. It had been right to reward the success of his first season, so, I guess, in the board's view, they were now acting on failure. But personally I was sick for Peter. I had worked very closely with him for many years, and I had never had an argument with him. We had had our heavy discussions, but certainly no blazing rows. I was on World Cup duty in America when I heard the news. It was a terrible blow.

I feel Peter Shreeve is in the Terry Venables mould as a coach and football man. When he joined the Queens Park Rangers coaching staff early in the new season the feedback from the Rangers players was that they were enjoying his ideas and his coaching style. Peter still holds his licence as a taxi-driver – just in case!

I think the Spurs fans may have resented the fact that Peter was not a big-name manager. Perhaps if he had enjoyed a stronger reputation he would have been given longer. It was his first shot at management, and while he is bound to be labelled a failure, I'm not so sure that he was. He was an unknown who had worked his way through the ranks. Had he been brought into the club, he would, I am sure, have been given a further year.

I also maintain that he was the right appointment at the time, even though he was not first choice. Alex Ferguson of Aberdeen and even Louis Cesar Menotti had been mooted for the job, but the decision to appoint from within was a sound one. In the past, it had worked with Keith Burkinshaw, and of course Bill Nicholson. I've heard all the sniping about Peter being a 'yes-man' for the board. Whether he was unduly influenced in the signing of new players, I wouldn't know. That's not the province of players. But I would certainly be amazed if the board had had any influence over him in team selection. I'm sure Peter was strong enough to resist any pressure of that nature. I remain convinced that Peter was left alone and unhindered to get on with the job of looking after the team.

The board operated a Continental system of management: the manager was solely responsible for the team, and the off-the-field problems, such as the renewal of players' contracts and the negotiating of transfer fees, were delegated to others. Peter was happy with that structure – it lifted the burden from a manager's shoulders and allowed him to devote his attention to the job in hand.

Peter was close to his players, but that should not be taken as a sign of weakness. He was strong with the players when he had to be. My only criticism would be that he was sometimes almost too calm and collected, too sedate and thoughtful. Sometimes a really good ruck or dressing-down is necessary. There were times in his second season of management when our on-the-field problems needed an immediate dressing-room airing. Instead we would always stick rigidly to the same format, which was to wait for the Monday morning inquest.

After a match, I felt we needed to get our gripes off our chests right there and then. I was sure, no matter how heated any arguments might have become, the exercise would have been carried out in the right spirit and would have proved useful. I suppose Peter wanted to maintain the policy that had worked well enough for him in the previous season, believing that it is wiser to wait for people to cool down so that criticism can be constructive than to allow emotions to override rational thought in the heat of the moment. I think, though, that a few more arguments would have got us going. By Monday morning everyone had cooled down, forgiven and forgotten.

Peter Shreeve was at his best in the dressing-room at half-time. He had the knack of spotting deficiencies and putting them right. He was on a par with Venables and Ron Greenwood in this. It is much easier to be destructive, but Peter always sought to be constructive. He was always on the button with his tactical changes. Perhaps he was wrong, at times, not to have had a real go at players but he could still be ruthless in some of the cutting remarks he made to them.

In public, however, he never criticised us. Instead, he would stand up for us in front of the media and, believe me, it takes a strong-willed man to face the Press after a 3–0 home defeat by Nottingham Forest, or after the crucial defeat by Everton. He was ready for the television cameras, he never shied away.

Peter was accused of being a 'media man', and to a large extent this was true. He spent far too much time with the media, and gave the Press far too much freedom to come down to Cheshunt. Most clubs believe in opening their training headquarters to the media on a Friday afternoon to encourage publicity for their home games. No one would have objected to the presence of the Press at Cheshunt one day a week, but they were there almost every day. It was open house for the media, and the players could have done without that.

The most distasteful and controversial factor in Peter Shreeve's sacking was a report in the national Press in which the manager and players were accused of certain indiscretions while they were in Jersey. I am not convinced that there was such off-the-field indiscipline that it cost the manager his job. I am quite certain that Jersey was used as a convenient excuse. Basically, Peter Shreeve was sacked because of what was going wrong on the field.

If we had been coasting at the top of the First Division, none of the Jersey business would have come under such close scrutiny. In my opinion the whole episode was blown out of all proportion. I suppose it didn't help when Clive Allen, who was driving a few of the lads back from a game of squash, was stopped by the police for speeding and reported. It all snowballed from there. Perhaps someone jumped on the bandwagon, and sold the story to one of the national newspapers.

I've had experience of this sort of drummed-up story getting out of hand. It happened to me some time before while I was on England duty when Ron Greenwood was in charge of the team. I ended up on the front page of the *Sun* newspaper, supposedly involved in a wild drinking session in a nightclub close to the Spurs ground when I should have been tucked up in bed at the England team's hotel.

I had gone out for a drink, that was perfectly true. I had gone with Kenny Sansom and Ray Clemence, perfectly true again. But the story made it sound as if we had lurched home at four in the morning. The truth was that we had gone out for a quiet drink with the approval of Ron Greenwood. He actively encouraged the players to relax and to go out on a

Sunday evening prior to a Wembley international, provided that we returned at a reasonable hour. We were back by 11.30 pm and, what is more, Kenny drank only orange juice all evening.

Similarly, the stories about Jersey were grossly exaggerated. As I have said, if we had been top of the First Division, I don't think the directors would have concerned themselves with the incident. It was no big deal. The harsh realities of soccer management are that success and winning are of paramount importance. That's not entirely Spurs' philosophy: our ideal is to win in style, but win nonetheless.

Finally, I have to pay tribute to Peter Shreeve for helping me at a crucial stage of my career. I had just begun playing for England, and Peter was Spurs coach at the time. The team had had a few bad results, and there was a big meeting. I was on the receiving end of a few strong words from Peter. He told me that I had changed since I had started playing for England. He warned me that I was being deflected from the game and concerning myself too much with outside activities. He told me it was about time that I started listening to people again, and that I still had a lot to learn. 'Instead of thinking about other things, you should concentrate on getting us out of this sticky patch', was Peter's hard-hitting advice. I thought about it deeply at the time. In retrospect, I realise just how right he was, and how wrong I had been. It was a vital lesson to learn.

I thought I could handle all my extracurricular activities, but I had got the balance all wrong. For a year I was in big demand off the pitch. I would do my training, shower, and be away from the training ground as soon as I could. I always had something to do. Peter got me to realise my error and I changed my attitude. Football comes first. I'm only likely to attract outside interest because of my football prowess. Peter reminded me that my main task must always be to stay on top of my game. So, instead of rushing away from the club, I began to stay to watch the youth team, to talk to the young players, and to contribute more to the club as a whole.

No one can blame a player for seeking earnings outside the game – the duration of his earning power is very short. He is a professional and must earn as much as he can over ten years or even less time in some cases. The security of his family is his priority, and that's why I was taking so much interest in the off-the-field activities. But I admit that I was taking too much away from my football, and had I not heeded Peter's sound advice I could have let my game deteriorate. After the lecture from Peter I swore I'd never allow that to happen again, and it hasn't.

I admire George Best for his exceptional skills and ability. He was one of my heroes – I loved his approach to the game. But sadly, George is an example to all of us of how not to do it. He demonstrates just how easy it is to ruin yourself and your talents. George Best's experience is a lesson to all players to invest their money wisely rather than lose it in a bottle. I owe George a lot for that lesson. Thanks George.

I also say thanks to Peter Shreeve. I pegged back on the commercial aspects and got on with my football, and I haven't looked back. Peter told me some home truths in front of the rest of the lads, and it made an enormous impact on me and on my life.

David Pleat

Spurs have changed under new manager David Pleat. The moment he stepped through the doors to replace Peter Shreeve he began to stamp his authority on the club. He decided to adopt at Tottenham the approach that worked for him at Luton.

It is a complete reversal of the climate that prevailed under the previous management. Peter Shreeve was very close to the players, and particularly close to me. It was easy to communicate with him. I find it difficult to understand David Pleat. He is a far more complex character than Peter Shreeve, and it is hard to know what he wants and what he likes. There's a touch of Brian Clough about him: an air of aloofness; a hint of mystery. Clough has had no trouble motivating his players through the years with those qualities. It will be very interesting to see whether that style of management will succeed at Spurs.

Pleat's football philosophies, however, are perfectly in tune with the Tottenham way, and his credentials are first-rate. He forced himself to the fore as the leading 'young' manager by transforming little Luton Town from the also-rans of the First Division into one of the best teams outside the elitist group of Liverpool, Everton, Manchester United, Spurs and Arsenal. He believes in good, attractive football, but I sense he has a ruthless streak. He wants to be a winner at all costs; he detests losing. He desperately wants to bring success to Tottenham, and I don't think he'll allow any players' reputations to stand in his way. Every manager likes winning, but David Pleat knows that a club like Spurs demands the big prizes in the game and that he has got to deliver.

Whether he is right or wrong, the new manager has been very positive in his approach. Changes came swiftly. He bought Richard Gough for £750,000, Mitchell Thomas for £300,000, Belgian World Cup striker Nico Claesen for £600,000 and 24-year-old England midfield player Steve Hodge for £650,000. He chose a squad of 15, maybe 16 players from the vast resources at the club, and the rest were out.

Mark Falco was sold off to Watford for £340,000, Graham Roberts to join Graeme Souness at Glasgow Rangers for £460,000 and Ian Crook to Norwich for £80,000. Paul Miller, Danny Thomas and Chris Hughton lost their places in the first team. Ossie Ardiles found himself fully fit after a long spell of injuries but unable, at the age of 34, to convince the new manager he was again worthy of a regular place in the team. He was used as substitute, and would no doubt only get in from the start in an emergency.

It is not for any player to question the manager's decisions. Every player has his own thoughts and preferences, but the game is all about opinion. David Pleat is perfectly entitled to follow his way of doing things, and it would be disloyal to question them. In my view, David Pleat is the right man for Tottenham: he has the right attitude and approach to the game. People have described him as the toughest manager the club has had since Bill Nicholson. Although I have been at Tottenham a long time, I was only an apprentice in Bill's day, so I cannot really make a fair comparison. All I know is that Bill Nicholson was a god at Spurs. When I saw him coming down the corridor, I would try to find an escape route, I would want to run away and hide. It will be difficult for anyone to follow in his footsteps.

This is not meant as a criticism of David Pleat – I am sure he'd agree with me when I say that he's still learning how to be manager of Tottenham Hotspur. There is a vast difference between Luton and Tottenham, and my instinct tells me that David Pleat is learning that fast. Any manager would be challenged by the transition from a small-town club like Luton to a big city team like Spurs, where the competition is fierce and the spotlight never leaves the club. A groin strain doesn't mean much at Kenilworth Road, but a groin strain at Tottenham is big news.

I'm sure he is now very much aware of the difficulties. There is no such thing as a private life at Tottenham. Everyone is continually under the scrutiny of the media. Once he has mastered all the outside pressures and problems, I believe David Pleat will emerge as a successful Spurs manager. He has a fine football brain; he is dedicated: he has a feeling for the game.

Personally, I have now come to realise that there is life after football. I need to get away from the game, to be with my family, play with the kids, or involve myself in a business venture – anything to take my mind off football for a while. It can become too intense, too overpowering. Football still remains the most important thing in my life, apart from my family and my faith, but I like to make sure there is a spell during the week when I think about something else and do something else. David Pleat watches a lot of games. He knows so much about so many players, even in the non-league sides. But you can put yourself under too much pressure.

Since Pleat arrived at the club, the results have not gone to his satisfaction or to anyone else's, for that matter. We've had quite a number of meetings to try to sort out the problems. Certain things have been thrashed out after a game, while other points have been held back until Monday for calmer analysis. There have been occasions when I've been puzzled by his reactions. When we have played badly, and would expect the manager to have a few strong words of condemnation, David Pleat has found one or two positive signs that have pleased him. When we have played well, and got a good result, something may have gone wrong to make him angry, or even lose his temper. Then he mulls over what has happened during the weekend and calms down. He is not an easy man to read, he thinks very deeply about the game.

A criticism that has always been levelled against previous Tottenham managers is that they have not known their best teams. The new manager has tried a variety of combinations in an attempt to strike the right blend and balance. He has taken a close look at what is a large squad of players and has made up his mind who will form the backbone of his team – and who can leave.

There have been rumblings that David Pleat is unconvinced about my style of play, and whether it has a place in the team he is trying to build. I'm 29 now and he has said that he must look to the future and experiment with alternative midfield partnerships. The issue of my future with the club became a matter for public consumption when the manager relegated me to substitute for the game at Norwich in 1986. All I can say is that David Pleat has given me no reason to doubt that he has faith in me. In fact, in all our conversations since he joined the club he has assured me that he believes in my ability and wants to encourage me to express myself.

Not long after I returned from World Cup duty in Mexico

where David Pleat worked as a commentator, staying at the same hotel as Bobby Robson's squad, the manager called me into his office for a chat. 'I want to play you in the Platini role', he told me. That is the sort of stuff I like to hear. He wanted me to have the freedom, just like the brilliant Frenchman, to go forward and not to have to worry too much about defensive duties. I'd always hoped a manager would say that to me. I was delighted. Unfortunately the new English Platini wasn't given a chance to get started.

The plan wasn't going too badly in pre-season until I developed a calf strain. The manager changed the system, switching Graham Roberts into midfield. I went with the squad to Barcelona for a tournament in the week leading up to the start of the season. The manager was quoted as saying that it would be a big test for me, that I had to prove my fitness before I would be picked. One national newspaper interpreted that as meaning that I faced the axe. On the morning the newspaper was published, word reached us in Barcelona and the manager had a reassuring word with me to confirm I was not on the brink of being left out. But I still had to prove my fitness because he was using only two players in the centre of midfield, Graham and myself, with Chris Waddle and Tony Galvin wide on the flanks.

Nothing was ever said about abandoning the Platini role, not even when I was finally dropped just three months after David Pleat's job began. Perhaps it was my fault. No one can get the best out of me with two in the midfield when I'm back on the edge of my penalty box. My strength is going forward. I know I can create chances for players like Nico Claesen, but not if I'm forced back to defend as much as attack.

I put the shackles on myself, really. The manager always maintained that he wanted me to go forward. I might have been wrong in trying to adapt myself to the new manager and coach and their system that had Graham Roberts and me in midfield. I should have asked myself 'why change?'. I've always stuck to my beliefs in the 12 years I've played in the

First Division. The problem was exacerbated by the fact that I wasn't playing well. I felt jaded after the World Cup. I had been playing for two years virtually non-stop, and I was in need of a break.

I always set myself high standards, and I felt I had peaked in the final 20 games of the 1985 season, when I was determined to clinch my place in the World Cup team. I desperately wanted to do well in Mexico, and the whole experience, the problems, the heat took their toll. There was bound to be a reaction. I had been inconsistent, and the manager had publicly criticised me for not getting forward, having shots and trying to score. Only Clive Allen was getting the goals.

The situation came to a head when we lost at home to Wimbledon. Unfortunately Wimbledon play in the style many teams are beginning to adopt these days. But if I'm on top of my game, it doesn't bother me who the opposition are or how they play, I can cope. I wasn't at my best, and the manager wanted to change our style, to try a new system with Gary Mabbutt moving out of defence into midfield playing alongside Graham Roberts.

Clearly, David Pleat wanted to see if Mabbutt and Roberts would function well in midfield without me. Since the manager had come to the club I'd hit my best form only in a couple of games. I would be the first to concede that it wasn't good enough. I don't blame him for dropping me – a manager has to do the job as he sees fit, whether he's right or wrong. David Pleat called me into his office on the Thursday before the Norwich match, and we talked over my problems. He told me he wasn't happy with my form, and I said I wasn't happy with it either. But I made the point that if he wants to get the best out of me, he has to play me in a certain way. Two in midfield just doesn't suit me at all. I told him it was no good keeping me pinned back on the edge of my own penalty area – that certainly isn't capitalising on my strengths – but that I was prepared to continue playing that way if he wanted. The manager said he wanted to look at something new. Had the new partnership of Mabbutt and Roberts worked, there might not have been any way back for me.

It was obvious that the decision to leave me out would be doubly controversial, coming as it did six days before England's big European Championship match with Yugoslavia at Wembley. We agreed that we would keep the news quiet. The manager said he would announce a squad of 15 names to include mine, and reveal his decision only when the teams were read out at 2.30 pm before the game.

But the news leaked out, which came as no surprise to me. I was banished to train with the reserves. There were a few people around at our Cheshunt training ground that day, including a couple of local journalists. It must have been a shock to everyone there to see me training with the reserves. After that training session the manager informed me that I would be substitute at Carrow Road, an issue that had until then been left open. It had looked at first as though I would be playing in the reserves.

I was not surprised to be left out. David Pleat had said that he knew what I was capable of doing, but that I wasn't achieving it, and in this he was perfectly correct. I was surprised to be named substitute. The team were a goal down at Norwich when I went on. From my position on the bench I had a vastly different perspective of the match. I thought to myself 'Sod it, if I come on here I'm going to do what I'm good at'. Perhaps I had become too relaxed as I got older. I was prepared to bend a little, and that was my mistake. Deep down David Pleat wanted me to express myself. After all, he had told me from the start he wanted me to play like Michel Platini! So, why not? It's not as easy as it sounds in the hurly burly of the First Division. But I know I have the ability to give it a go.

Almost immediately I helped pull a goal back and we looked as though we might win the match. I was sure I could help the team more by using my individual abilities rather than by concentrating on defensive duties and skills.

When I played for England at Wembley on the following Wednesday night in the European Championship game against Yugoslavia, I was not out there to prove David Pleat wrong. I set out determined to prove Bobby Robson right. Between the Norwich game and the international, I had continually been asked about my future. David Pleat had been quoted as saying he would sell me if the price was right. He added that any player at any club has his price, but that part got lost in the Fleet Street translation. In the popular Press, shades of grey don't make very interesting stories or eye-catching headlines.

The interpretation was clear. Pleat was prepared to sell me if the right offer came along. My response was to say that I'd be prepared to go if the right offer suited the club. I felt that such a reply was reasonable, although it was a difficult situation. Certainly, I had nothing to prove to the England manager. It had taken me the past two years to build up my position in the team.

International football suits me, and I was delighted to have had a good game against Yugoslavia. The clash of heads with Steve Hodge made me out to be some sort of hero, but I had been in the game long enough to know that I would be a hero one day and knocked down another. I have learned to take the knocks one day and the adulation the next without going overboard.

Not long after our clash of heads, there was a meeting of minds as Steve Hodge and I teamed up at Tottenham. I must admit I was surprised that Graham Roberts was sold to Glasgow Rangers. Obviously, Graham was sold to finance the purchase of Hodge, but the ramifications of Graham's departure won't be known for a little while, until we see how the manager's reshaped team works out. The team pattern has changed yet again since he left. In my view, Graham Roberts is a smashing player to have in your side. He has been a good servant of the club and we got on very well off the pitch. I think he's at his best at the back, even though he was switched to midfield by David Pleat. His best years at Spurs were spent in the back four as a central defender.

Graham's only problem was his temperament. He needed

to be calmed down on a few occasions during games. He would get over-heated, and I have had to tell him not to overreact to referees and opponents. Graham was susceptible to being wound up by opponents. He would carry on conversations with the opposition, and because of his reputation, he would go into tackles and come out 'back-chatting'. I would tell him to forget it and get on with the game and to keep 'doing his stuff'. But he seemed to enjoy the verbal confrontations with players, and that didn't help his cause with the officials. But he was vastly different in training: he was sensible; he never got involved. He respected the fact that it was training, and he never indulged in any full-blooded 50-50 tackles.

I was also a little taken aback by the manager's farewell comments about Graham. I'm sure his remark that Graham would be going to Rangers to kick a few in Scottish football after kicking a few down here was meant to be tongue-in-cheek, but I have a suspicion that part of David Pleat knew his comments would be used, that people would jump on the old bandwagon and use that sort of remark as ammunition to have a go at Graham. I didn't think it needed to be said.

It came as no real surprise when Steve Hodge was signed from Aston Villa. He had been talked about as a likely transfer target ever since David Pleat arrived at the club. Steve has a nice left foot, a lot of energy and scores goals from midfield. We're not similar players, but I'm sure the manager is looking ahead in his rebuilding plans over the next few years. That is certainly the right approach for the club.

Another of the manager's changes was the appointment of Richard Gough as skipper on New Year's Day at Charlton. David Pleat wanted an outfield player to skipper the side, and it seemed only a matter of time before Richard would take over. I rate him as a player, but he does have problems, now and again, against a big centre-forward. He is a good, footballing centre-half and has more ability on the floor than Mike England, but he's not as dominant in the air. I like the way Richard keeps possession when he wins the ball.

7
Soccer's Hidden Dangers

Precious few footballers have ever dabbled in drugs, particularly hard drugs. Players, especially those in the top bracket, are earning big money – more than the Prime Minister of this country – but the vast majority are still working-class lads. The drugs scene is alien to them. Of course, a few may mix in the wrong circles. The jet set that love the fashionable West End nightspots will now accept the professional footballer, and some of the young men with fat wage packets are sometimes tempted by the bright lights. If that happens, though, their clubs quickly bring them back down to earth.

Drugs are prevalent in the more aristocratic sports such as tennis, one of my favourite games outside football. Athletics is riddled with performers taking steroids or other complex drugs to improve their capabilities. But football as a sport is not conducive to drugs, in the sense that drugs would be more likely to impair a player's performance than to improve it. Players' union leader Gordon Taylor is fully aware of the pressures in professional football. There have been players, under severe stress, who have resorted to pill-popping, perhaps taking tranquillisers to ease the tension, and then 'uppers' to wake them up come match day. But even these cases are few and far between.

I have put my name to a campaign to deter youngsters from taking drugs. I'm sure every professional footballer in the country would back such a campaign. Problems with injuries can lead players to take drugs. Inflammatory tablets are often used to help the healing process, and painkillers and a variety of injections are commonplace. The stress of losing a promising career prematurely is one of the biggest danger areas. Months or even years of fighting injuries can affect the psychological pattern of a young man who suddenly finds himself on the soccer scrapheap.

Paul Vaessen was once a bright prospect with Arsenal. He scored the winning goal late in the European Cup Winners' Cup semi-final at Juventus having come on as a substitute. A bad injury finished his career, and he turned first to soft drugs, and eventually to heroin. Paul ended up fighting for his life in hospital after being savagely attacked, allegedly over a row concerning payments for drugs. I naturally feel a great deal of sympathy for Paul. I hope his fortunes improve. But happily there are few cases like his, and I don't know of any players currently in the game who are involved with hard drugs.

Drugs are totally alien to footballers, who are generally down-to-earth characters. They have a wonderful lifestyle, and I cannot imagine why anyone would be stupid enough to risk losing it through taking drugs. The FA introduced random drug tests a few years ago, and no one has yet been discovered taking drugs. I'm sure it would be impossible for anyone on drugs to fulfil the physical demands of a 90-minute game. You wouldn't need to carry out a drug test, anyone could see it for himself.

The worst pressure to me would be not having a job. It is scandalous that there are millions unemployed. I have a wife and two kids to support, and I would not jeopardise their welfare and my future by experimenting with drugs. Anyone on drugs in professional football would be regarded as an outcast, a cheat, not only to himself but to his profession. He would be a disgrace to the rest of us and would also, I am sure, be ridiculed.

A year before the World Cup finals, the England squad was in Mexico acclimatising. We stayed at the Camino Real in the heart of Mexico City. One evening, out of sheer boredom, Kenny Sansom, my room-mate, and I decided to play a trick on Terry Fenwick. We phoned Terry's room and his room-mate, Dave Watson, took the call and handed the phone to Terry. At the other end Kenny and I put on American accents – Kenny is a superb mimic and I had to disguise my voice as well as I could. Terry, thinking he had a crossed line, was astonished to discover that he was listening to a conversation between two American guys discussing a drugs shipment.

'Hey, Tony, have you got the drugs?', I said in attempt at a Chicago gangster-type of accent.

I handed the telephone over to Kenny. 'Hey man,' he said, in a brilliant imitation of the same, 'I've got it, and I'm talking about 100 kilos'.

We were falling about, desperately trying not to burst into fits of laughter. We never thought for a minute that Terry would fall for it. 'Hey, man, there's someone on the line, I'm splitting', spluttered Kenny, slamming the phone down.

The next day, Kenny and I just couldn't stop laughing. Terry hadn't said a word, but Dave Watson was sure he had fallen for it. When we all sat down for lunch, Terry was next to me. Suddenly he just had to get it off his chest. He turned to me and started telling me and all the other lads about the call he had overheard the previous night.

'You won't believe what happened,' he began, 'there were these two American gangsters dealing in drugs – in this very hotel! I heard them on the phone.' Well, we couldn't contain ourselves any longer. We burst into laughter. The tears were rolling down my face. Terry's face dropped. He'd been slaughtered!

The joke we played on Terry Fenwick goes to show how removed the world of drugs is from football. In my opinion, the real addiction in the game is gambling. In moderation, betting can be an absorbing pastime, but regrettably, a number of players have suffered and are still suffering badly from what must be seen as an 'addiction' to gambling.

I would be the first to admit that a small flutter is harmless fun. In fact, it can even be beneficial. Most soccer teams have their own card school which provides a form of relaxation before matches, and it can help to build team spirit by getting the players closer together. When the England squad played in Russia shortly before the World Cup finals, the card school was going non-stop. It was a way of killing time, and we needed to in Russia! Kenny Sansom and I normally pair up and play against Peter Shilton and his partner. When Peter Beardsley first joined the England squad he knew only Chris Waddle, from his Newcastle days. We had never met Peter, but we soon got to know him through the card school. He started off as the 'puller', helping somebody else. We got to know him far quicker than we would have done otherwise through the humour of the card school, where Peter sat next to 'Shilts' and joined in the banter. However, I have heard about one club banning their card school: the players were betting heavily on the cards, which led to bad feeling and negative reactions. It only takes one bad apple in the school, one bad loser, for things to get out of hand. There is certainly no trouble of that kind at Tottenham, or with the England group. The England lads are smashing, and we have some great fun.

I enjoy a day out at the races, either horseracing or greyhounds, and a lot of players feel the same. For me the horses are an interest, a pleasurable hobby. I go to the racecourse knowing beforehand that I will lose £60, and I have £60 worth of bets on six races, no more. But gambling can get out of hand with some players, taking a grip on their lives. There are players who cannot pass the High Street bookies without diving in and betting heavily. I have heard of one or two players who watch television minutes before they trot out for a game, to see their horse line up for the three o'clock race. At half-time they are sometimes more interested in how their horse fared than in the state of the match.

Footballers are very vulnerable to the gambling bug. They earn big money in a short space of time and from an early age. They are away from home and thus from the influence of their families. They have far too much time on their hands. Some of them urgently need sound advice.

Gambling becomes a danger when a player can no longer handle it, loses heavily, and the worry begins to affect his form on the field.

To stay at the top in football you have to live with pressure. It is certainly a vastly different sort of pressure than that caused by being on the dole or working down a coal mine, but it is dangerous to add to it the strain of trying to cope with a gambling habit. We all enjoy a drink after a match – players are only human. They like a few drinks to help them relax. But some just cannot escape gambling: racing is on the television every day, and betting shops are everywhere.

Whereas on a social day out at Ascot or Newmarket I might, as I have said, put £10 on a horse, some players might bet £1,000. I wouldn't like to put that sort of pressure on myself. If you're going to lose £1,000 a time on a regular basis, it is going to hurt. There can be no doubt that gambling will ruin a player's career.

Oddly enough, although I love horseracing and the dogs, I am actually petrified of animals themselves. In spite of this fear, I once came very close to buying a horse in partnership with Alan Brazil. Alan joined us from Ipswich, and although he didn't have a successful Tottenham career he was long enough at the club to forge a close friendship with myself and Graham Roberts. The three of us shared an enthusiasm for horseracing. A few times a season we would all have a day out at the races.

Alan and I soon decided it would be a good idea to buy a racehorse. Alan knew all the trainers and felt sure he would find a bargain. So we went to Newmarket, to a stud farm owned by Clive Brittain. Alan sought the advice of Jock, a vet who knew quite a bit about horses. We examined three potential purchases, but the first two didn't look at all good. The third, which Jock recommended, was absolutely massive. I had never seen such an enormous animal in my life. As I'm very wary of animals, I was not at all keen to get too close, I can tell you. This brute looked like Albert Steptoe's horse

Hercules. To have any chance of winning a race, it would have had to have been castrated and run over hurdles.

The price of the horse, called Cradle of Jazz, was £2,000. It didn't seem to me a wise thing to do to part with £1,000 each for such a shabby-looking creature. I don't think Alan was too keen either in investing his share. We went to a nearby hotel, had a few beers, and thought it over. The more we talked about buying this horse, the more we went off the idea. When it became clear that we were not going to go through with it, we began ridiculing the poor animal. 'There's no way we're going to buy a horse that could double as Steptoe's', I told Alan. We rolled about with laughter to think that we had nearly parted with £1,000 each for that huge, tatty-looking thing. But somebody was daft enough to buy it – and it won its first three races!

Looking back, we could have won enough money to have paid for that animal in the first few months. I bet it is running to this day, knowing our luck, and still doing well. It hardly needs to be said that we are not very good judges of horses, and luckily, we didn't go through with our plan to look around for another horse. We would probably have settled eventually for an absolute beauty, and never won a race. Just look at our judgement over 'Steptoe' – he didn't look as though he could have managed to walk around the course, let alone run.

When I was five years old I was badly mauled by an Alsatian. I went over to the dog to stroke it and it jumped up and scratched my face. I was clawed just under the eye, and had a nasty scar for quite a while. My Mum told me the story about the dog: it's not something I remember vividly, even though it sounds like a scary experience. But that attack has had a lasting effect. Whenever there is a dog around, I have one ear on the conversation and the other on the dog. You would never think, knowing this, that not so long ago I bought myself a greyhound called Chris's Babe for £500. I wanted the greyhound to be named after my wife Anne, but it would have cost another £200 to change its name. Now, don't get me wrong, I'm not mean, but I drew the line at £200 to change a dog's name. In any case my wife's full name is Christine Anne, so we compromised with that!

I bought the dog in partnership with a close friend of mine, Barry Crouch. She originated from Ireland and had a fine pedigree. I went to examine the dog, and it was a great feat for me to actually stroke it. It was just a tiny puppy, and it looked so harmless that it was hard even for me to be afraid of it. Chris's Babe was a lovely looking dog. I was very excited when she was taken to the dog track by her trainer for her first taste of the traps and the track.

There were two other trialists there and Chris's Babe was excited too. She went berserk in the traps. Around came the hare, up went the trap doors and out flew the two trialists . . . but where was Chris's Babe? The other two dogs were halfway round the track chasing the hare, still we waited for Chris's Babe. Suddenly a little head popped out of the trap, had a look around and dived back in. 'Oh no, I've just spent £500 on this dog', I thought to myself, 'and the damned thing can't even run out of the traps.' It took 40 minutes of prompting before the greyhound got the hang of it, and understood that she was supposed to chase the hare.

The big night of Chris's Babe's first run at the Walthamstow track attracted my Tottenham team-mate 'Max' Miller and wife Shelley, myself and Anne, and Barry and his wife Carmel. It was only six weeks after the first training session that had gone badly wrong. Not surprisingly, our trainer thought she had no chance of winning, and from what I had seen thus far I completely agreed with him. I figured if it came in fifth it would be doing well. But she was running from trap one, which increased her chances.

We had all had an enjoyable meal watching the dogs, and so I decided to have £25 to win on Chris's Babe, which was more of a sentimental bet than anything else! Even 'Max' Miller, who doesn't bet at all, had £25 on Chris's Babe.

Would you believe it? That dog shot out of the traps, led all the way, and won by three lengths. We were all on our feet, cheering the dog all the way home. The Chandlers, the owners of the Walthamstow dog track, gave us a wonderful memento of our dog's first-time win, a lovely greyhound in a bottle on a stand.

Chris's Babe carried on racing, and I believe did very well. I haven't kept up with her progress, really, as my partner Barry took responsibility for her. I'm sure she has retired by now.

8
Glenn's Golden Goals

There was a spell when every goal I scored seemed to be quite stunning. I couldn't say that those goals were the result of planning, they were simply intuitive. I once heard a radio commentator describe my goalscoring, and his observation has always stuck in my mind. 'Glenn Hoddle is not a great goalscorer,' he said, 'but he's a scorer of great goals.'

I have scored something like 120 goals for Spurs and for England, and the majority of them have provided me with a huge amount of satisfaction. Forwards pile up their goal tallies with little two-yard knock-ins. I rarely get among those sort of strikes. And my favourite goal? Well, that must be the one I scored against Manchester United at White Hart Lane in the 1979–80 season. I'm sure quite a few people will know the one I mean. It was repeated often enough on the television, and I must admit I still get a great deal of enjoyment whenever I see it. I feel proud and fulfilled to have created something special.

The goal came after Terry Yorath played a free kick to me, my back to goal. I flipped the ball round the back of the defender and played a pass to Ossie Ardiles. The superb, skilful little Argentinian returned the compliment with a perfectly weighted pass and I volleyed from the edge of the box on the angle into the roof of the net.

So many people have approached me and said that I must have spent hours on the training pitch with Terry Yorath and Ossie Ardiles practising that free kick move. Well, we could have tried to practise it, but we would probably have abandoned the plan as totally unworkable! The truth is that such a move is 100 per cent off the cuff. It couldn't have happened any other way. It was a once-in-a-lifetime goal. Terry Yorath looked up as he stood over the ball ready to take the free kick and played the ball to me. The sequence of events just moved on from there.

I think I have scored many spectacular goals in my time, and I hope that doesn't sound conceited. But that goal gave me more enjoyment than any other. It was such a breath-taking move and the finish was as sweet a volley as I've ever managed for a goal. I felt sheer exhilaration when the ball went in. Lovely! Unbelievable! My emotions raced, but I didn't celebrate in any special way – I don't have a Mick Channon windmill action!

That was my favourite goal, perhaps even the best goal I have ever scored. But there is one that comes very close to it in my affections and in my ratings, and that is the one I scored on my England debut against Bulgaria at Wembley. The date was 22 November 1979, and the game was one I will always recall with pride and patriotism. There I was, at the age of 22, playing in front of 71,000 people at Wembley in a European Championship match. It was the first time I had been called into the full squad, and I would have been delighted to have been among the substitutes. On the coach returning from training on the Tuesday I learned I was in the team. Ron Greenwood simply got up at the front of the team bus and read through the line-up – and my name was in it!

We had already qualified for the European Championship finals. Ron Greenwood had allowed Kevin Keegan to return to West Germany, so my room-mate Kevin Reeves also made his England debut. We won 2–0, Dave Watson scoring the first, and I put away the second. The ball flew across the face of the penalty box and out to Trevor Francis on the right, I shouted and he laid the ball inside for me. I had thought about blasting the ball but there was a defender chasing me so I decided on a side-footed shot from 20 yards.

I suppose, technically, that sort of thing just isn't done. It's not in the soccer manual. I side-footed the ball because I wanted to make sure the shot was accurate, but once again it couldn't possibly have been planned. I didn't make up my mind about how to play the ball until I reached it.

The ability to side-foot a shot with power is something that can be practised, but it is a skill that comes naturally to me. I term it 'passing the ball into the net'. When you blast the ball, one day it will fly into the roof of the net and the next it will zoom out of the ground. In training we used to have sessions devoted to 'finishing', and I have seen many players who are able to side-foot their shots from 20 yards with power.

The goal I scored against Bulgaria was extra special because I caught the ball with the side-foot on the half-volley. That's a more complex technique. But as far as I was concerned the strike was not a one-off. I was striking the ball that way in the Tottenham youth team, so I knew I had the ability to score with a side-foot shot, and I knew I could hit the ball with power, even on the half-volley. But it was something special to bring everything together on my England debut. It was a goal of distinction, and I am delighted with it.

Bobby Charlton was a scorer of fantastic goals. Perhaps he was not as great or as prolific a goalscorer as Jimmy Greaves, but his goals were often out of the ordinary. He chose to blast the ball and he did so with great accuracy. Yet for every impressive goal Bobby Charlton scored with his powerful shooting, I'm sure another shot went over the top. I've seen Clive Allen master the skill of shooting with power and accuracy with the side of the foot. In fact a lot of lads at Spurs perform the technique in training, when the ball is on the floor. It's more difficult on the half-volley. The knack is all to do with timing to get the power from 20 yards or more. I scored another goal with a side-foot into the corner against Leeds that pleased me.

I suppose the goal that has become a trademark of mine is the free kick around the edge of the opponents' penalty area. The goal I scored from this position against Wolves in the FA Cup semi-final is one I recall with great relish because of the importance of the occasion. The goalkeeper ran across to take a position behind the wall, believing I was going to curl and chip the ball over the wall. Instead, I sensed the move made by the 'keeper, so I curled it into the opposite corner.

You do need a sixth sense with these free kicks. Once my head goes down, I'm watching the ball and can't possibly know what the goalkeeper is up to. Of course, I take a peep a split second before I go to strike the ball, but once I'm committed to taking the strike my eye is on the ball, and my head is down. I don't really know whether the 'keeper has decided to stand his ground or to anticipate a chip over the wall. It is handy to have the reputation of being able to curl the ball into either corner at these free kicks because the goalkeeper and the defence tend to over-compensate for the possibility of a chip over the wall and the defenders are encouraged to commit themselves to that side, leaving the other corner an easy target.

One goal from a free kick that I remember well occurred at Mansfield during our season in the Second Division. I have a video recording of the goal which helps refresh my memory. It was an awful day. There was a downpour and there was hardly a blade of grass left on the pitch. I had scored from a penalty, but we were still 3–2 down in one hell of a game.

When we won a free kick outside the box, the ground conditions were so appalling that I had to put the ball on a mound I made out of the mud. With just 30 seconds of the game left I curled this free kick over the wall and into the top corner. Once again, I believe that the technique to curl a free kick, a speciality of the Brazilians and top Europeans, comes naturally, but it is a skill that can be practised on the training ground.

Over the years, I have tried to pit my skills against some of the best goalkeepers this country has produced. Peter Shilton is the best 'keeper I've faced yet, curiously, I seem to have a good goalscoring record against him. The first goal I scored in top flight football was against Shilton.

In August 1975 I made my senior debut against Norwich at White Hart Lane, coming on as a 20th-minute substitute. Cyril Knowles limped out of the game with a knee injury, and although no one knew it at the time, of course, it was an injury that ultimately put him out of the game for good. I came close to scoring. I flicked the ball over a defender's head, then volleyed it on the way down and it flew just over the bar. I was pleased with my performance in a 2–2 draw, John Pratt and John Duncan being the scorers for Spurs.

I was substitute a couple more times, but it wasn't until the middle of February 1976 that I finally got my big break with my first full game for Spurs. I travelled to the Potteries to face Peter Shilton and Stoke at the Victoria Ground. We had lost 3–0 to Queens Park Rangers the previous week, and Terry Neill dropped Terry Naylor and Ralph Coates, bringing in me to wear the No 7 shirt, and Mickey Stead at right-back. We won 2–1 and I scored the winning goal, opening my account against the one and only Peter Shilton.

The ball had run loose of a defender 25 yards out and I heard John Pratt yell 'Hit it!'. I did. It was a sweetly-hit, angled drive that lifted into the net. It was a great way to start, especially as my whole family had travelled up there to see me. I have continued to score against Peter. I have had a few against Nottingham Forest in my time, but that left-foot drive against him on my debut is still one of the best goals I have scored against him. I have kept an old tape of that goal for posterity as well.

It still wasn't *the* best goal I have scored against Peter, though I celebrated my 22nd birthday with a really special one that was chosen as 'Goal of the Season' on television. It came only a month after my 'best-of-all-time' goal against Manchester United, in the second round of the League Cup, and I scored it with a right-foot volley against Forest. Once again this was a special goal – the ball never touched the ground from the time it left the boot of our goalkeeper Milija Aleksic.

Aleksic kicked a long clearance downfield, Gerry Armstrong

flicked it on, Chris Jones pushed it back to the edge of the box and I smashed it in past Peter. It was after that that Keith Burkinshaw said I only seemed to score spectacular goals. I'm not sure whether he was complaining or not!

That was some season. I scored on my England debut, and I finished top scorer for my club with 19 in the League, including seven penalties, one in the League Cup, and two in the FA Cup. Largely, no doubt, as a result of this success, I won the Young Player of the Year award in the annual poll run by the Professional Footballers' Association. Terry McDermott of Liverpool won the Player of the Year award, but I learned afterwards that only the voting system prevented me from taking the top prize. The votes for me from my fellow professionals were split, some cast in the senior category, others in the young player bracket. Twenty-three goals in one season. I'd like to be able to score that many now, but I feel my game has changed.

In that season we didn't play what I would call 'good' football, as we did in, say, the season we won the FA Cup. We got the ball forward far quicker and it was inevitable that I would end up on the edge of the opponents' box more often. We had players like Steve Perryman, John Pratt, Ralph Coates and Terry Naylor. The style was not to play too much through the middle. There was no need for me to be the playmaker in midfield. I prefer to be more involved in the game. It may surprise quite a few people but my preference is to create goals rather than to score them, even the spectacular ones.

There is as much satisfaction to be gained from creating a goal as from scoring. I would expect people to look back on my career and pick out my creative abilities as my top attribute. Creating is my prime function, and goalscoring is secondary – a bonus, albeit a very pleasant bonus.

Besides my favourite goals I remember with pride and affection the best goals I have created. I made all four goals against Feyenoord in the UEFA Cup tie at Tottenham. All of them came in a blistering first half. The team was in scintillating form, and my passes were setting up goal after goal.

Johann Cruyff was playing that night, in one of his last big matches in Europe. I have always been an admirer of Cruyff's special skills, but I didn't put on any sort of show for the Dutchman. It was an important game against one of the top teams from the Continent. At the end of that match I came off the pitch as satisfied as if I had scored all four goals myself.

To select the best goal of my career was a difficult enough choice, but to recall the one pass that gave me most satisfaction is even harder. I suppose the one that comes to mind took place, again, in an important game and at a crucial time. It was the FA Cup semi-final against Wolves at Highbury. I hit a perfect long-range pass with the outside of my left boot into the path of Garth Crooks, who raced on clear of their defence to score.

I mustn't forget that I have scored some goals with my head: not many, of course. So few in fact that I know exactly how many – eight. My best header came in a 2–2 draw with Crystal Palace. I scored our first with a side-foot volley from 12 yards out, and for the second one I came to meet an identical cross, but this time I produced a firm header. I have also scored with my head against Millwall and Norwich, where I've been pretty pleased with myself. And more recently I nearly scored my first international headed goal when I struck the post against Northern Ireland in our opening European Championship match of the 1986–87 season at Wembley.

From the age of eight I have always been my team's top scorer, and always from midfield. At junior level, they would always put their best young player into midfield. I never copied anyone else's style, I developed my own. As far back as I can remember the skills, the techniques were there, and I never had to work to manufacture them. Everything seemed to come so naturally. I believe the key has always been timing.

In retrospect, it surprises me that I have such natural gifts. I am delighted, of course, but surprised. At the time, it never occurred to me that I was so lucky, but I certainly realise it now. I have always been able to stroke the ball around with the outside of the foot, and to chip the ball with back spin to land at the feet of a forward-running player. Although I have never modelled myself on any other player, I have seen some of the great players that are capable of chipping the ball forward with back spin, such as Franz Beckenbauer.

I have noticed the way some players have picked it up from me. Steve Perryman realised how it could be done, and I saw the technique appear in his game in the way he started to pass the ball. He tried it for himself and it came off. Steve Perryman is a good user of the ball, he very rarely gives it away. When he played as a sweeper during our season in the Second Division he looked a much better player. He showed that he can produce the sort of techniques that few people realised he had, probably those skills he gave up at an early age when he first came into the Tottenham team and was asked to perform a specific function in that team.

I was a schoolboy when Steve Perryman arrived on the First Division scene. He was an adventurous player to begin with, but then he became known as the team's midfield runner and ball-winner. However, in the latter stages of his career, maybe through watching players like myself and Ossie Ardiles, he has reverted to a more adventurous style.

From a purely personal point of view my most memorable match for England was the 3–0 win in Hungary. I scored from a free kick, curling it over the wall. I won't forget the 1986 Wembley game against Yugoslavia in the European Championship and my clash of heads with Steve Hodge – the scar on my forehead won't let me! My most satisfying game for Tottenham would have to be my performance against Feyenoord. We have had some great nights of European glory at White Hart Lane, but that was a night of high personal satisfaction, too, since I created all our four goals in a marvellous first-half performance. The game to trump them all would have to be the FA Cup final replay with Manchester City at Wembley in 1981. What a great game! It was a privilege to be involved in such a match. It had everything: goals, drama, excitement. Ricky Villa's goal must be one of the best ever in a Wembley Cup final. The game looked as though it was slipping away from us, so it was gratifying to finish on the winning side. The way we snatched victory was quite remarkable.

As well as the high points of my career there have been, of course, a few lows. Particular disappointments are my two sendings-off. Both were a result of stupidity on my part, and I deeply regret them. The first was at Crystal Palace. I scored that night from a free kick and I was enjoying a good derby game. Then, as I was getting away from Jerry Murphy he pulled me back by the shirt. I swung round in annoyance, and we finished squaring up to each other. There were no punches thrown – it was more like handbags at ten paces! It was strange really, because I had been desperate to play in this match. I had rested for a couple of games because the combination of a hamstring injury and poor form and results meant that Keith Burkinshaw and I felt it would be for the best.

But I didn't like the idea of missing the League Cup tie with Palace and I asked to return. I felt good in the match, scored our equaliser and began to run the game. I've always admired Bobby Charlton, not just for his brilliance on the football field, but for his exemplary behaviour and disciplinary record, or lack of one. So it was depressing to be sent off for the first time in my career. I had wanted to go through my career without a single major blemish. I was annoyed with myself, but not with Jerry. I couldn't blame him for pulling me back: I had broken through and might have gone on to score. In fact, Jerry and I are good friends. We spent the remainder of the match standing at the head of the tunnel watching the Cup tie, chatting away to each other, telling each other how stupid we'd been and discussing where we would go afterwards for a quiet drink!

I was sent off for a second time in very similar circumstances. I had been out of the game for a long time with a serious Achilles' tendon injury, but once again I was eager to play, this time even more keen than for the Palace match. I came on as a substitute against Bruges in a UEFA Cup tie ending a seven-month lay-off. All the frustrations and the worries about whether I would ever play again had been building up. Now, I was back on the football field, and I was really keyed up.

I had been playing for no longer than a couple of minutes when Tony Galvin was pulled down. When that sort of thing happens to me I get up, walk away from any trouble, and get on with the game. For some strange reason, no doubt something to do with all that pent-up emotion, I reacted. In fact, I overreacted. Tony was on the floor, five yards from me, and I went over and pushed the guy who had brought him down. The referee booked me. Well, I hardly deserved that, but I suppose I only had myself to blame for getting involved in the first place.

At last I got comfortably into the game, getting hold of the ball and beginning to feel like my old self. It was terrific. Then there was a foul on Mark Falco, and the ball came spinning out to me and I hit a pass from midfield, just as the referee blew for a free kick to our side. My natural instinct was to chip the ball down the line as I saw John Chiedozie making the break, but he stopped running immediately he heard the whistle. It must have appeared to the referee that I had deliberately kicked the ball downfield to waste time, which certainly was not the case. But it didn't matter too much about the rights and wrongs of the incident – he showed me the red card. Sent off again! I couldn't believe it. Another sorry tale of stupidity.

There have been some lighter moments. I have played in goal three times for Tottenham – and not once finished on the losing side. The first encounter of the goalkeeping kind occurred in a League game at Leeds. We were a goal ahead but our 'keeper Barry Daines was clobbered by big Ray Hankin after about 25 minutes. Barry was knocked out cold in the collision and was carried off. Everyone looked around at everyone else. No one fancied going in goal, and who could blame them? Leeds were always a tough side, they rarely took prisoners. We had just seen our 'keeper flattened – who wanted to risk that happening to them?

In the park as a kid I loved to go in goal. Midfield was always my first love, but sometimes it took my fancy to try out between a jacket or a jumper thrown on to the ground. So I said that I would have a go in goal. It seemed a brave offer at the time, but I was really scared stiff. I tried not to show it. I wasn't frightened of any physical contact I might have to endure, I was more worried about knowing exactly what I should be doing and when, scared of making a fool of myself.

I wasn't in goal for too long, about ten minutes, before I was already picking the ball out of the back of the net. But, hold on a minute, don't think it was my fault! No one was pointing the finger at me. There had been a corner, a shot was blocked, the ball ricocheted to Trevor Cherry six yards out and he smashed it past me. I had no chance. It was from this sort of set piece that I was at a loss technically. I didn't know what sort of position I should be taking up.

At the half-time interval there was a general panic in the dressing-room. I calmly took our coach, Pat Welton, to one side in a relatively quiet corner. Pat used to be a goalkeeper and he specialised in coaching 'keepers. 'Look,' I said, 'come over here a minute and explain to me whether I should be at the near post, far post or in the centre of the goal at corners'. Pat Welton gave me a crash course in goalkeeping techniques and off I went, very relieved.

In fact, I made some excellent saves in the second half, if I say so myself. My confidence grew and I even came out for some crosses. I think my defence began to stop panicking and as the team relaxed a little more we went up to the other end and scored. Our supporters were massed behind my goal in that second half. We had a large contingent of travelling fans that day, as we usually do when we play away from home. I got some terrific support from them. But, quite naturally, there were plenty of jibes from rival fans, and I was pelted with coins. Fortunately none hit me. We won that game 2–1. It was a strange sensation coming off the field at the end wearing a green jersey!

Even though we had come away with a notable victory and I had played my part in it, I had not really enjoyed it apart from the final 15 minutes when we were ahead and it looked as though we were going to win. I was just glad to get through it. It was more survival than satisfaction – I was thankful to have escaped without embarrassment.

The next time I went through the ordeal of playing in goal I really enjoyed the experience, although you would have thought it would have been more terrifying, for the stakes were that much higher. It was our vital FA Cup tie at Manchester United. Perhaps the knowledge that I'd been in goal before helped me, not just to get through it, but actually to relish the task. I knew I could cope, having gone through it all before I had no qualms about taking on the job. I was able to display my 'goalkeeping talents'!

All the more satisfying was our extra-time victory with an Ossie Ardiles goal. His effort is often recalled on television. He looks as though he doesn't have the energy left to run but he glides his angled shot from just outside the box into the far corner. The execution was superb – a great little chip. I went into goal about 20 minutes into the second half when Milija Aleksic found himself in terrible trouble after a clash with Joe Jordan. But as the match resulted in a goalless draw, the game went into extra time, and I made a save that not only was I proud of, but also helped the team to win this important Cup tie.

We had gone into the lead and were hanging on in extra time when Ricky Villa tried a tricky back pass from a corner, chesting the ball down in my direction. That was a bit too clever for my liking, even with a regular goalkeeper, and I certainly wasn't too impressed when it happened with me in goal, especially since we were hanging on desperately for a place in the next round. As Ricky played the ball, and I don't know why he took such a risk, in nipped United's Steve Coppell, just eight yards from goal.

He was lining himself up for a certain equaliser. I remember thinking 'He's going to smash this one in'. I dived at his feet, spread my body as wide as I could – just like a real goalkeeper! – and hoped for the best. The next thing I knew, the lads were congratulating me on a great save. In reality, the ball had hit me on the arm and shot by the post. I had my eyes shut at the time, but I suppose it must have appeared an impressive save!

I heard the crowd cheering, but I knew that if Coppell had chipped the ball it would have gone over my body and been a certain goal. That 'save' gave me extra confidence. So much so that I had the nerve to pretend a goal-bound 'bullet' header from Gordon McQueen didn't really cause me any trouble.

McQueen has a habit of standing as close to the goal-line as he can manage when a corner is floated under the bar. United won a corner and they used this ploy with McQueen standing virtually on top of me. The idea is at least to unnerve the goalkeeper. The corner was floated to the edge of the six-yard box, and I went to punch it away. I hesitated, fearing I'd miss it, and I was caught between going for it and going back to my line. McQueen got their first and his header smashed against the bar, and must have rebounded 20 yards. 'Where were you', I was asked, probably more in jest than anything else. Quick as a flash I came back. 'If I thought it was going in, I'd have gone for it', I replied nonchalantly. 'I had it covered'!

That incident didn't deter me from going for crosses. Once, I spotted big Joe Jordan baring the gap where his two front teeth should have been and wearing an expression that clearly meant 'I'm going for this cross and I aim to get it'. 'Go for this one, Hod', I encouraged myself. Up I went and the ball stuck in my hands – I couldn't believe it. But, as I came down, I dropped it. Three of our defenders and three United lads all converged on the loose ball on the six-yard line.

However, I wasn't finished yet. As the ball dropped out of my hands I bounced it with one hand, bounced it round one United player with the other hand, practising my basketball dribbling skills while our defenders held their hands over their faces, hardly daring to look. At the time, the lads gave me quite a bollocking, although later, in the dressing-room, they seemed to have changed their minds. I'm sure they thought it was hilarious afterwards. I wish I had – I'd been in a state of panic, I'd scared the living daylights out of myself.

I know everyone thinks that goalkeepers are slightly mad – I'm sure they are. But I enjoyed my experience. There were even lighter sides to that evening's work. The Stretford End crowd warmed to me and refrained from throwing things at me, which was a relief. But someone did throw one object – a tennis ball. Fortunately it didn't strike me, it simply rolled past me, so I picked it up and volleyed it back into the crowd, which got a laugh from the fans. It was the first thing I had kicked straight all night!

Perhaps my most vivid memory of that match was the moment that Milija Aleksic went down injured. He was clearly badly hurt. It was an appallingly wet night, and the poor bloke had to be stretchered off. Of course, I felt a great deal of sympathy for him later, but at the time the extent of my compassion consisted of yelling to our physio, Mike Varney, 'Get his gloves!'. There was Milija being carried off in agony and all I could think of was getting his bloody gloves off him before he went. It sounds cruel. But that was instinctively my main concern as feelings of fear swept over me. Milija Aleksic had been in trouble again when I went in goal for the third and last time. With around 20 minutes to go at Norwich, Milija jumped to punch clear a cross, but he landed on one of the hooks inside the net and ripped his thigh open. Once again he was carried off. This time we managed to get his gloves before he was put on the stretcher! I had scored to put us 2–1 ahead two minutes before Milija left the field.

9
Perils on the Pitch

A professional footballer's body takes a battering from head to toe during the course of a full career in the game. The worst injuries are those built up over a number of years with the continual twisting and turning of the ankle and knee joints. A cartilage or ligament operation can be as dangerous to a player's career as a broken leg. The Achilles' tendon is obviously one of the areas at greatest risk.

I have suffered my fair share of injuries, but it is a complete fallacy that I am injury-prone or that I cry off from matches at the merest hint of a knock or a twinge of pain. In fact, the statistics suggest that the opposite is true. Only five players in Spurs' history have made more appearances than myself. I have played more than 500 times for the club, often turning out far from 100 per cent fit.

I know I have a reputation for moaning about my injuries. My answer to that is to recommend a look at the records of the games that I've played. If Joe Bloggs gets injured, it doesn't make news. But if Trevor Francis, Bryan Robson or I are out through injury, it's blown up into headline news. The public's reaction must be 'Oh, he's injured again!'

Football is a very tough sport. The joints can take quite a pounding from the general running, twisting and turning, and the fact that it is also a contact sport means it can be very physical at times. Tackles, in addition to the twisting, put the joints under enormous pressure. Apart from the routine bumps and bruises, I have run up a long list of serious injuries.

The ankles are constantly under attack. Six years ago, I

was kicked on my left ankle, one of the worst kicks I ever had. I twisted at the moment of impact. My big mistake was to play on despite the injury. It had occurred in the first 20 minutes of the game. For this type of knock, a spray is used to freeze the area, killing the pain, so sometimes you are just not aware how bad the injury is. I finished the match but I soon regretted it – the ankle joint swelled badly. I was sidelined for six weeks with badly strained ankle ligaments.

By far the worst injury of my career was to the left Achilles'. The problem built up over a period of time as long as three years. It was wrong to have continued playing on it. The problem is that the crowded programme of fixtures doesn't give you any time to rest. I really needed a long break, but that just wasn't possible and finally, the only solution was an operation. This was the only time I really feared that my career might be over, and it was a difficult period for me. I've had problems with the right Achilles' too, but they've been minor compared to those with the left one.

In my time I've had to endure close man-to-man marking. I've been deliberately hacked down, pulled back and generally kicked about. But you haven't heard me moaning about that. However, there have been a couple of exceptions to the normal wear and tear of football that I feel have every right to protest and complain about. Reuben Agboola caught me just above the left knee when we were playing Southampton at the start of the 1986–87 season. It was a particularly nasty tackle that resulted in my being stretchered off. I had twisted knee ligaments that needed to be immobilised in plaster for two and a half weeks, and in the end I was out of action for seven weeks.

The most vicious incident I could hardly call a tackle – it was more like an assault. The guy should have been charged with grievous bodily harm. It was 12 December 1984 when we played Bohemians Prague in Czechoslovakia for a place in the UEFA Cup quarter-finals. We drew the match 1–1 to go through 3–1 on aggregate, but I was stretchered off.

Jakubec Sloup was the villain. He hit me with everything

he had. It was the most outrageous tackle I've ever come across. He kicked me so hard, with almost the whole of his body, that I wound up with a painful 'dead' leg, a bruise at the top of the knee, a gashed forehead that needed 12 stitches and concussion. The wound was stitched by our club doctor in Czechoslovakia but had to be reopened and stitched up again when we got back home. Graham Roberts also collected a nasty cut in the head in that brawl of a match. It was the thigh injury that kept me out for a couple of weeks.

That experience helped me, in a funny sort of way, when I split my head open in a clash with Steve Hodge against Yugoslavia at Wembley in the European Championship match in November 1986. I was half-screening the ball as I bent down and kicked it away from an opponent. I was leaning as the guy spun me around, and the next thing I knew I had crashed into Steve Hodge. As I collapsed to the ground holding my head and feeling the blood, the first thought that ran through my brain was the memory of that episode in Czechoslovakia. I looked over at Steve and he was flattened too. The game was still in progress.

I checked my eye. I was concerned as the impact had been so close to the eye. I put my finger right into the hole – the blood was gushing out. Because the eye was all right, and because of my previous experience, I did not panic as I had done in the Bohemians match. Norman Medhurst was the first on the scene. He told me that I would have to come off. The wound was serious and I was still pretty shaken up. I got to the bench and told Bobby Robson that I was quite willing to go back on if it was medically OK to do so. Steve Hodge had been carried off and we had already used one substitute.

Fred Street put a huge bandage around the wound. It was much wider than a Steve Foster headband, and the only problem was that it went right over my eyes! I told Fred that he had better cut two holes in the strapping so I could see where I was going. He said there was no need for that, and lifted it up. Even so, I could hardly see.

Apart from other minor cuts and bruises I've suffered the

odd groin and hamstring strains and pulled muscles. I had a cartilage removed at the age of 15 and at that stage my career could have been over before it had started. I was with Spurs at that time and they provided the best surgeon and medical care. Because I was tall and gangling in my youth I also developed some back trouble but that cleared up before the end of my teens.

The big problem with regard to injuries is to decide when a person is fit enough to resume playing. There are precious few professional players in these days of overcrowded fixture lists that are 100 per cent fit every time they perform. There are occasions when a manager is so anxious for a particular player to be ready that he will ask that individual to have a painkilling injection to enable him to perform for the duration of the match. Kevin Beattie complained that running too many risks and having too many injections contributed to his downfall.

There was one occasion when I was persuaded to play with the aid of an injection. An opponent trod on the top of my foot, making a hole which needed three stitches. The only way I could play the following week was by having the whole area frozen with an injection. I tested the foot on the morning of the game. I was willing to play even though it was still a bit sore. In the fitness test, I kicked the ball with the problem foot. That was about the measure of the fitness test. The final decision has to rest with the player – he is the only one who can really know the extent of the injury, the only one who can judge the damage.

Some players do try to con the manager – it depends on the game and how badly the player actually wants to play. Only the player knows how his body feels and how it will stand up to the strain. For a World Cup tie or Cup Final, it's certain that a player will consider taking risks, particularly if there are no more games afterwards and there will be a long rest period. I played in a game at Luton a couple of years ago when I shouldn't have. A kidney and rib injury made me very doubtful, but I made the mistake of deciding that I was all right to play. I had had an injection to deaden the pain, but I knew in the fitness test that my movement was restricted. Instead of complaining, I played. It was a total blunder on my part. I knew as soon as I ran out on to the pitch I wasn't right, and that there was no way I would perform to my true potential. I thought it was wise to say nothing, and no one knew the truth.

Throughout my career I have played with injuries. Our former skipper Steve Perryman had a reputation for playing through the pain barrier, getting on with the job despite his injuries. It would not surprise me if I had played as many, if not more times, when I was injured than even Steve Perryman.

As you move forward through the team a player can expect more punishment. Defenders are usually dishing it out, and in midfield or attack you are on the receiving end. In midfield there is a lot of close marking, and with it comes physical contact. In my younger days I never wore shin pads, which was a big mistake. I would urge all youngsters playing the game to wear as much protection as possible. I've discovered shin pads that I wrap up around the ankle, more like cricket pads than football shin guards, and for extra protection there are four plastic strips inside the elasticated guard in addition to the padding at the front. Tony Galvin simply can't wear shin pads. I've never seen shins like his – they are riddled with scars and marks. One kick was so bad it turned poisonous – you could press your finger into the wound and make a mark. He tries to wear them now, but usually discards them early in the game. He says he doesn't feel right in them, and he's not alone in this. Some managers, though, will fine a player who refuses to wear them.

Plastic pitches are a menace. I don't like the surface at all, it's not conducive to good football. It can also cause injuries. You can get nasty burns by sliding on the synthetic surface. But the real danger is the constant pounding on the hard surface, which puts more pressure on the ankle and knee joints. The only advantage, in terms of injuries, is the footwear worn on these pitches. There are no studs used, so even

Tony Galvin would be reasonably safe without his shin guards! Studs are also dangerous when it comes to twisting and turning. If an ankle or knee goes one way, and the stud catches in the ground and twists the body in the other direction, cartilages and ligaments are placed under extreme stress, and can tear or even snap.

There can be no doubt that I've been kicked more times than I've kicked opponents, but there have been occasions when I've regretted clobbering an opponent. Mostly it has been accidental, but there have been a few occasions when an opponent deserved to be kicked. In one game my old mate and England colleague Terry Butcher was making a defensive clearance for Ipswich and as he belted the ball virtually out of the ground, I put up my foot in an attempt to block the ball. Terry cleared the ball but my foot came down and 'studded' him just above the knee. I apologised to Terry – a wise decision as he's bigger than me! He sustained a nasty cut above the knee, and I deeply regretted what had happened. I blamed myself, in a way, although I knew the blow had been unintentional.

If an opponent marks me tight in midfield, I view it as a challenge to get the better of him. I want to make my superior skill pay off. I have reached a stage in my career where I believe in my ability to get the better of such situations. I am able to cope much better than in the past because I've come to terms with the fact that you have to meet force with force at times. Once you've matched an opponent on that level, you have cancelled each other out, and if that's all he's good at, my extra skill will come out on top. World-class players like Pele and Maradona have had to endure close marking. They learned that they had to stand up for themselves, and that lesson has been driven home to me in the last few years.

10
My Faith

At the age of 18, I did something totally out of character that was ultimately to have a profound effect on my life. As a shy teenager I plucked up the courage to walk over to an attractive girl at the bar of one of my local pubs in Harlow and offer to buy her a drink. I was on an evening out with a few of my mates, and the girl was sitting with a couple of her friends.

I may have been reasonably well-known in the locality, but I wasn't an instantly recognisable footballer. I had only just got into the Spurs first team, and there wasn't a queue of girls waiting to talk to me. I had seen Michelle before and thought her very attractive, but I hadn't found the courage to talk to her until that night. I suppose I'd known her by sight for a couple of years. I hadn't even said 'hello' before.

We started to go out together and got on quite well. One night I went round to her house and met her Mum, Eileen Drewery. Two weeks later I went back to Michelle's house again after we'd been out somewhere. I had been having treatment with our club physiotherapist, Mike Varney, for a hamstring injury. I was walking with a slight but noticeable limp, and the injury was quite sore. This was a Thursday night and it looked as though I had absolutely no chance of playing on the Saturday, and Mike felt I might be out of action for a fortnight.

Michelle's Mum noticed my limp and asked what the trouble was. I explained about the hamstring injury. We sat down and talked for a while and Eileen offered some 'healing'. Michelle had never mentioned anything about her Mum being involved in 'healing', and I laughed. Eileen asked me what the matter was. I'm sure she was a little taken aback by my reaction. I told her: 'Well, I don't really believe in all that, I don't understand it'.

When I look back at that first encounter 11 years ago it was amusing. I honestly believed that I would have to take my trousers off, and I was very embarrassed. I'd known Michelle and her Mum quite a few weeks by now, but I didn't think I knew them well enough to take my trousers off in front of them! I expect that's why I tried to laugh it off.

Eileen explained to me that I didn't have to believe in faith healing for it to have a benefit. She suggested that I tried, or rather that she tried, 'absent healing'. I really didn't have the first idea what she was talking about. I went into the kitchen for a cup of coffee with Michelle and spent some time talking away. As I was going home, Michelle's Mum said: 'Don't worry about the leg, it will be all right in the morning'. I laughed again. 'Oh, I'm sure I will be all right', I said as I left.

I woke up on Friday morning and got out of bed . . . I couldn't feel any more pain in the hamstring. I remember sitting up in bed, digging my finger in as far and as hard as it would go, searching for the pain. It had gone. I was absolutely staggered! That's the only way I can describe how I felt. I rushed to the phone and rang Michelle. 'What's happened?' I shouted. Michelle said: 'Mum did some "absent healing" on you while you and I were in the kitchen last night'.

I found it all very hard to take in. I reported for treatment that morning at the ground and had to explain everything to Mike Varney. I was afraid that the club would think I had been faking an injury to avoid training. Mike Varney was very understanding. He had a pretty open mind about faith healing. He didn't say that he believed in it, but he refused to run it down either. He just advised me to keep it quiet, which I did. At the end of the day, he was pleased that my hamstring injury had been cured. I was bemused, but I really didn't think too deeply about it.

But over the next 11 years, I went back often to see

Eileen. Even though I had broken off my relationship with Michelle after about eight or nine months I have been back many, many times for healing sessions with her Mum. At first I didn't see Eileen for a long, long time after she 'treated' me. She moved out of the area, began work in pubs and moved around quite a bit. It was through mutual friends involved in local Sunday League football that I discovered that she had moved to Hatfield. As it was such a long time since I had last seen her, I was too embarrassed to call her myself. It was through the prompting of my Mum and my wife Anne that I finally got in touch with her again. My Mum telephoned Eileen, and I went over to Hatfield to see her. I had a thigh injury. I hoped she could do the same with the thigh as she had managed with the hamstring.

It is hard to explain, but I felt I was using her. I didn't understand what it was all about. I thought I was the only one to benefit. I was wrong, but it took me a long time to discover the truth – that Eileen benefited too, that she wanted to heal people. As far as I was concerned I just thought how lovely it was for my injuries to go away just like that. I was still not really thinking very deeply about the true meaning of what was happening. Whenever I went to visit Eileen for treatment we talked about football, about the pub, but we never spoke about the healing.

The process was simple. Eileen would ask me to relax and I would get comfortable. I shut my eyes mostly, and would even nod off to sleep. I took very little interest in what was going on. Eileen would also relax and then lay her hands on the injured part of the body. She didn't say anything (it was only later on that I discovered that inwardly she was praying). To me, it simply looked as if she were concentrating hard on the injury. I got an intense feeling of heat. Her hands always became too hot.

Eileen moved back to Harlow, oddly enough to the pub where I first spoke to Michelle. I had been suffering with an Achilles' injury over the years, and Eileen tried to heal me without success. She felt that I would have to have an operation. She sensed it, and she was proved absolutely right. After the Achilles' operation I was out of the game for such a long time that I began to doubt that I would ever play football again. Eileen helped me to overcome those fears.

Periodically I've popped back to see Eileen and her healing has always worked for me. At the beginning of 1985 I had problems with my right Achilles'. I saw her five times, and she cured it. In January 1986, I went to see Eileen with a knee injury. At about this time I was beginning to feel that there was something missing in my life.

It's not easy to express in my own words just how I felt at this time. I hope you, the reader, will understand what I'm trying to say. I shall do my best. I couldn't quite put my finger on what it was I was actually missing in my life, but when I looked at certain people, like Eileen, Cliff Richard and other people I'd heard on television talking about Christianity, I realised that there was a different life to the one I was leading at the time. I thought hard. I wanted to have what these people had got, even though I wasn't totally sure what it was.

I'd always had a fascination for Eileen and her healing powers, but until then I had not bothered to consider them profoundly. She was interesting to talk to. I began to notice more acutely how much she cared and her consideration for other people. I was beginning to feel compassion toward my fellow man. I began thinking very deeply about a lot of things. I started with little prayers. Perhaps they were more thoughts than prayers. I didn't know if I was praying or not.

I began to think that I would like to live a life like Eileen, or indeed Cliff Richard, with a purpose, a meaning to it. But I was confused. I thought it would take a drastic change, so drastic that I couldn't see myself doing it. I had only felt like this once before in my entire life. That was five years before. I was invited to a 'Christians in Sport' dinner at the club. Cliff Richard was there that night. Did Cliff have an effect on me? Well, yes and no. He did in the sense that I went away from meeting and talking to him and tried to read some books, including the Bible, but my confusion didn't leave me.

I tried hard. But the penny didn't drop. I really didn't understand what I was reading. I read Cliff's own book, which was a more modern way of putting things than the Bible. I started reading the Bible but it went over my head. Yet, I did feel there was something missing from my life. I could see it in people like Cliff Richard, but somehow it was eluding me. I wanted it, but I couldn't grasp it. How could I when I didn't know exactly what I wanted? I put down the books, I didn't pick them up again. I stopped reading and went back to the way of life I'd always known.

I suppose when I analyse what was happening to me the only way I can explain it is with the word 'confusion'. The confusion came in the feeling that I would have to change the whole of my life. I liked going down to the pub with my mates to enjoy a drink or two, I'd tell jokes and listen to them. Would I have to change my social activities? I didn't know. It was as if my life in the scheme of things was somewhere in midfield between good and bad. I didn't consider myself a particularly horrible or bad person, nor was I a believer in anything. I felt as if I would need to make an enormous jump from my middle ground to reach the sort of faith I was seeking. From halfway to the other end of the scale was a gap I didn't feel I knew how to breach. I didn't know how I'd have to change socially, or change my family life, and then there was the added problem of working in the environment of professional football. I was a little envious of those people who had found faith in their lives. Well, perhaps envy is the wrong word. It was unobtainable, out of reach, too far away. It was frustrating. I didn't believe I was capable of changing my way of life dramatically enough to enable me to live according to the Christian way of life.

I had tried it before when I first met Cliff Richard. I failed then, and I thought I was going to fail again. I'm sure other people, too, may have tried it, and not made it the first time. It was around this time that Bobby Robson's squad assembled for one of its World Cup warm-up games in Israel. Feelings were bubbling up within me, but I wasn't making any headway. Even though I was seeing Eileen something like twice a week at this time, I never discussed my thoughts and feelings with her. These feelings, I suppose, were at a sort of 'teething' stage. They coincided with our game in Israel.

The day before the game the England squad went on a tour of Jerusalem. We visited the Wailing Wall and then went by coach to Bethlehem. We saw the place where Jesus was born. We went through a small door at the side of a huge castle and church built on top of the site. It was inside a cave that we saw the actual birthplace. It just seemed right being there. There was strong spiritual sensation.

I remember leaving the cave and the church and feeling uplifted. Perhaps I might have felt like that anyway, even if I hadn't visited the birthplace of Christ. For the previous six weeks or so I had been praying in my own way and thinking about my faith. I could have walked out of that cave, like the rest of the England lads, and thought that it was a fantastic experience to see the birthplace of Christ. But there was something more. I experienced a very strong spiritual feeling . . . that this was right. *This is right*. Just being there and considering the historical life of Jesus.

If anything the experience helped me in the game the next day. I still felt uplifted when I returned home. It just seemed the timing of that trip to Israel was perfect. Everything that had been happening to me before fell into place. It has become such an important part of my life that I decided to tell the story, just as it happened, in this book. When I look at my notes, I've jotted down: 'Was this a coincidence or was it fate? To go there at a time when I was seeking something else from life'. But I noted again: 'I still feel confused'.

There were still many things in my mind that I needed answers to. I began to realise that it all stemmed from Eileen and her influence. I visited Eileen about my knee problem which was still troubling me after the Israel game. I was playing on, but the pain was lingering. Eileen was baffled, even staggered, that her healing had not cleared up the knee injury. In the past, all her healing had worked apart from the one time when I needed the Achilles' operation.

Despite all my visits, all the years I'd known Eileen, this was the first time that we talked, really *talked* about my feelings and thoughts about life and faith. The conversation got round to the trip to Jerusalem, and to Jesus's birthplace, and the thoughts I'd been harbouring for the past couple of months. I said to Eileen: 'It's funny that I should go to Jerusalem at the time I had just started to pray a little and think of things I used not to think about – and those feelings have become very strong'. She told me: 'That's exactly what faith healing is about. It comes from God, not from me'. For the first time I thought of God being involved in healing.

Eileen's powers of healing came from God. She believed in Jesus Christ. I wanted to discuss if further. Was the reason I kept going back to her for nearly three months with this knee problem that I would eventually get into a discussion about praying, and faith? I began to believe that it was meant to be. Eileen explained how she felt her healing powers came through God, and we have had many long discussions on the subject. That has helped me enormously. I felt a strong compulsion to go back to her, and now I knew it had nothing to do with my knee.

I surprised Annie one day when I asked to go to Church with her. I had not told Anne anything about what had been happening to me. Anne's a regular Churchgoer. I think she was shaken a bit. Going to Church was another uplifting experience. My faith grew stronger. Perhaps I'd been searching all my life for something that was always meant to come to me. I'd been searching, now I'd found it. I may have found it, but I'm still learning about it. I discuss it with Eileen whenever I can and I've spoken with our local Reverend.

All those questions I was asking, and I found the answers – myself. My prayers were really asking for guidance. And I discovered it was possible to obtain the Christian life I had seen in others without dramatically changing my way of life as I had first thought. I was still in the process of talking with Eileen and other people when it was time to leave for Mexico and World Cup duty. On the other side of the world, I felt a little cut off.

Anne rang me in Mexico and must have guessed how I felt. She had been rummaging around the house looking for a book on baby food (the latest addition to our family, Zara, was about five months at the time). In a drawer, Anne came across Gerald Williams' book *A Whole New Ball Game.* It had been given to me by Harry Hughes, who runs the Spurs Shop, at the time of the 'Christians in Sport' dinner at the club five years before. That book could easily have been thrown out, but it hadn't. And I was so glad that it hadn't. It was written for sports people, men and women who have discovered a new life in Christ.

Anne wondered if the book could help. She opened it at random and there was a chapter on Alan West, the former Luton player who had turned to Christianity. It explained a lot of the things I had been going though. Was that yet another coincidence, or was it meant to be? After the World Cup finals I returned home and read that book. I was able to relate to it because it was a book about sportsmen and women in a similar situation to mine. I found a lot more answers to the questions that had always bothered me. I was sure I was meant to read that book at just that time. It was a great help after the isolation in Mexico, where I prayed daily for guidance. There had been no Eileen, no going to Church with Anne. It was good to be home.

Gerald Williams' book was an inspiration. He showed me that tennis players, boxers, cricketers and footballers had found the answers they were seeking. The confusion had disappeared. I realised I didn't have to make that huge jump. God comes into people's lives in different ways. It doesn't matter if you're a sportsman or whether you have a strict religious background. Now my faith got stronger and stronger, by the day. My life had changed.

My outlook on life is completely different now. My feelings towards others have been transformed. I don't think I was a bad person before, but my faith in God has made me a more caring, compassionate, patient person. I'm loving and caring towards others, not just the wife and kids. I pray for others. There has been a big transformation in my life. Life is so much fuller. I feel there is more of a reason for being on this earth than just to live your life out.

I now go to Church on Christmas Day, which I have never done before. That's just a small example of how my life has changed. I go to Church on Sundays, but I don't feel as though I have to go to Church every single Sunday – I would be letting my faith and myself down.

I still have my ups and downs in business and in football, and I might have a period of bad form. But I know I have not been put on this earth just to play football. I lead a great life: I make a good living from football; I have a nice house, a car, all the material things anyone could want from life; a lovely family and friends, two wonderful children, a lovely wife – everything. Why, you might ask, did I feel as though something was missing? It sounds as if I want everything. But now I know that before I didn't have everything, and that the 'something' that was missing really is the most important thing in life.

I have by no means turned a bit weird or cranky. My life hasn't changed dramatically on the outside, just inwardly. I wouldn't force my views on anyone, but I hope that, indirectly, some people may be helped by my own struggle to find the truth. I feel better able to cope with a lot of things that might have got me down or depressed me in the past. I feel we are here to get along together as people. For example, when I was dropped by the manager this season I was able to handle the situation. Before I would have dealt with the problem in a completely different way. It's the same with injuries: they no longer get me down.

Now I know what it is I had been looking for in people like Eileen and Cliff Richard: the uplifting sense of fulfilment; caring about and loving other people. This new feeling is a wonderful thing – if anyone thinks I had everything I wanted before, they're badly mistaken. I hope you will understand what I'm trying to say. If anyone reading this is experiencing the same sort of confusion I went through in trying to find their faith or something new in life, then I hope that my struggle is of help to them. People find their faith in different ways, and there are many ways of finding God. If you are searching I hope you find what you are looking for. I'm sure you will discover it in your own way and when you are ready, the way I did.

I just can't believe how lucky I am that it has actually happened to me. I value it much more than all the material things I have always had. I must admit if I'd heard a story like this in my younger days I'd have been sceptical. Now I understand how it has become possible.

11
Opportunity Knocks

You do not have to be a football connoisseur to realise that my style is best suited to the Continental game. I have never really believed that I fitted in in England, and I have taken criticism of my style and my attitude. I have wanted to play abroad from the age of 21, not simply because I wanted to escape from the bondage of English football, but also because I have always felt that the Continental style would be more conducive to bringing out the best in my game.

I am basically quiet, even shy with people, and I tend to keep myself to myself. I'm a family man. But that doesn't mean I lack ambition and drive – far from it. I want to be the best, and perhaps the only way to prove it was to move away from Tottenham to Italy, West Germany or Spain. I felt that if I had not tasted the game abroad by the age of 30, following in the footsteps of Kevin Keegan, Liam Brady, Ray Wilkins, Mark Hateley, Gary Lineker, Mark Hughes and others, I would have been kicking myself.

At the age of 29, I felt it was probably my last chance to fulfil my burning desire to play abroad. I don't know if I will ever be regarded as the best and to be honest I have to say that I doubt whether I'll ever be totally accepted in Britain. I know people are divided – they either love me or hate me – and even my own managers at Tottenham have had their doubts. Keith Burkinshaw, for one, never hid them. He publicly slated me for lack of effort and commitment to the team, a criticism that has stuck.

In England I would wake up in the morning knowing I could do more with a football than most other players in the country. I don't play a careful percentage game, and I am ready to take risks. I admit that sometimes I attempt a 'killer' pass when most players would play safe, and most managers would want me to play it simple. But I believe in free-flowing, exciting football. I wanted to be entertained when I was a kid on the Tottenham terraces, and now, in turn, I want to entertain the fans. I also want to be a winner.

It used to upset me when people had a go at me, but not any more. I have become a harder, tougher character; I am more resolute. The deep concern about my Achilles' injury made me realise that I would be throwing an awful lot away if I didn't give everything I've got to my performances. I have always maintained that I am capable of making an impact in the England team, given a fair run in the side. That never happened until I recovered from my injuries and Bobby Robson picked me non-stop for the year leading up to the World Cup finals, a year in which England remained unbeaten. Playing for England only increased my conviction that I would be better suited to the Continental game.

Perhaps the closest I came to quitting this country before I finally moved to Monaco was at the age of 21. I even brought forward my marriage to Anne a year to make certain that the move would go through smoothly. I was lined up to follow Keegan's trail-blazing path to the Bundesliga, and I could have signed for either Schalke or Cologne. My contract was running out at Tottenham. It is amazing how well informed clubs, even foreign clubs, are about players' contractual obligations. They plan their moves so that they can step in when a player's contract is about to expire. One day, a fellow who called himself Felix turned up on my doorstep in Harlow. He told me that he had arranged the Keegan transfer to Hamburg, and asked if he could talk to me.

I wasn't yet a full international. Even so, he talked in telephone numbers. When I went to Austria with the England squad I was approached again in my hotel, and talks took place. A negotiator and his lawyer met me out there and persuaded me that I could earn staggering amounts of money.

Nobody but my room-mate Graham Rix knew what was going on as I sneaked away for hush-hush talks right under the noses of Fleet Street's finest football reporters.

Kevin Keegan was extremely helpful. As he had experienced life in West Germany, I took the opportunity of going on the England trip with the under-21s, who shared a coach with the senior squad, so that I could ask the advice of the England skipper en route. He told me how much he had enjoyed playing for Hamburg, but emphasised that he left to play abroad only after he had established himself as a full international. The old England centre-half Dave Watson, on the other hand, had a miserable time with Werder Bremen. I'm sure he would have painted rather a different picture of Germany had I asked him. Nevertheless, after my chat with Kevin I was as determined as ever to go.

I can still hardly believe how lax Spurs were throughout this period. You would have thought that they would have been wise enough to open talks with me to sign a new contract long before my old one expired. Not at all. I hadn't talked to them, and they did not talk to me, about renewing my contract until the old one had virtually expired. As the rules require they sent me a new offer in the post. (Unless a club offers a player terms that are at least equal to those of his previous contract, the player is available on a free transfer.) I returned their new offer unsigned, and it wasn't until shortly before we returned for pre-season training that Keith Burkinshaw called me into his office to discuss the situation. I told the manager that he could not persuade me to stay. I had made up my mind to play in Germany.

But in spite of my determination to further my career in Germany I came to the realisation that the time was not right. One morning I woke up and I had changed my mind. It still seems strange when I remember how committed I was to going, but I simply changed my mind, for no reason I could put my finger on. Perhaps I just wasn't ready. After all, I was only 21, and although I had been thinking about the move for some time, at the back of my mind there was always this nagging doubt that I was too young, I was being too hasty. There was plenty of time. The temptations were enormous, though – I was being offered tremendous amounts of money.

I'm a great believer in fate. In retrospect, I realise that I was too immature and inexperienced to play on the Continent. My wife Anne was disappointed – she had been sure her A-level in German would finally come in handy! It is amazing how time flies by in football. It seems like only yesterday that I decided it was too soon to go abroad. When it looked as though my opportunities to play on the Continent were running out, my determination not to let my last chance slip by in the summer of 1987 increased.

When I was ready, willing and eager to move abroad – about four years ago – I suffered the worst injury of my career. Around Christmastime, it looked certain that AC Milan would wrap up a deal for me. The Milan club wanted me to replace Belgium captain Eric Gerets, who had, ironically, been troubled by injury all season. Once again my contract was up for renewal at the end of the season, and once again I was getting nowhere with manager Keith Burkinshaw.

In February, I went to play for England in Paris. It was suggested that Hamburg and Barcelona would take this chance to watch me. The Hamburg manager, Gunter Netzer, had made it known that he would be in Paris, and was quoted as saying: 'Hoddle is our number one target. We want him to do what Kevin Keegan did for us. There is a great opportunity for him in West Germany'. Napoli and other top Italian clubs had made contact with my adviser and these facts were reported at the time, but I myself knew very little of what was going on. I preferred to concentrate on my football.

This time, however, I was ready for a move, and I would certainly have gone through with it. There would have been no turning back, no last-minute doubts. But once again the fates were against me. I had been playing on despite the Achilles' problem, which was getting worse and worse. Finally, it became too much of a burden. I had an operation in April, and that put an end to any possibility of going abroad. There had been a lot of interest, but nothing concrete. I was 25 years old and about to hit my prime, but instead of switching to the Continent, I signed a handsome four-year contract with Spurs.

The reason for this long commitment was that the club wanted to put an end to the constant speculation about my future. They didn't want me to sign another two- or even three-year deal which would have caused the question to crop up again.

The headlines claimed that the four-year contract was worth £1 million – I wish it was! It was nowhere near that amount. Nonetheless, the club showed tremendous loyalty towards me, considering that an Achilles' injury is among the worst a professional footballer can have. Spurs had elevated me to the status of one of the highest-paid players in the country and I was determined to fight my way back to fitness as much for them as for myself.

When I returned from World Cup duty with England, I heard that there had been interest once again from abroad. But I have to be honest – there was nothing really serious. My ambition and determination to play abroad had not died – on the contrary, if anything it was now stronger than ever before.

The 1986–87 season was the penultimate year of my four-year contract. But in view of my 15 years' service, the Spurs management and board were big enough to let me go willingly. Before the appointment of David Pleat in succession to Peter Shreeve, I sought a meeting with the club chairman, Irving Scholar. It was after our last game of the season, before I was due to leave with England for the World Cup. I asked the chairman if he would release me if he received an interesting offer from abroad. I told him I still felt it would benefit my game if I played on the Continent. The chairman's reaction delighted me. He said he would wait to see exactly what offers from which clubs materialised and then he would make up his mind. I was given the clear impression that the club would not stand in my way provided that I was leaving to improve my career.

I am sure the chairman wanted me to go only to one of Europe's best and biggest clubs. He had my best interests at heart, and he also knew that there was little point in keeping a frustrated player with unfulfilled ambitions. Furthermore, it made financial sense for Spurs to cash in on my talents at that stage of my career.

I was very much aware of my priorities. I knew nothing would come my way unless I had a good season. It was not easy at the start. I had been playing a lot of tough games in different conditions in Mexico, and I was pretty jaded at the start of the season. I'm enough of a realist to know that, in life, you don't always get exactly what you want. So, when no opportunity arose for me to go to Italy or Spain, I chose France – and I have not looked back.

I had a purely personal desire to try something new for my career – whether abroad or in Britain. Every now and again people need an injection of new life. I had had offers to play for some of the biggest clubs in the country, deadly rivals to Spurs, such as Arsenal, Manchester United and Forest.

When my previous contract was coming to an end, right out of the blue I received a telephone call at my home from Brian Clough. He spoke with an air of confidence and said that he was interested in signing me for Nottingham Forest. I was very flattered. I have a lot of respect for Clough and the prospect of playing for him certainly appealed. He was very honest with me and said that it was entirely my decision. I had still not recovered from my Achilles' tendon problem, and I seemed destined at that time to stay at Spurs.

I thought the chance to play under 'Cloughie' might turn up with England. At one stage I thought it might be on the cards that he would become England manager. Another slim chance to play for him arose a little later when he made an inquiry about taking me on loan to Forest. But it was a cheeky move, and the club turned it down.

Clough's first, and more serious, approach came about the time I had talks with Arsenal. Terry Neill, who had given me my debut at Spurs, was then manager at Arsenal. Out of courtesy I had talks with him – I'm always prepared to listen to any offers.

The ex-Manchester United manager, Ron Atkinson, has said on television that I was one of the first players he tried to sign when he arrived at Old Trafford. In fact he was more than serious. I met him in a Luton hotel when my previous Tottenham contract had expired and he told me he wanted to build his side around me. This was before he spent £1.6 million on Bryan Robson. He wanted to emulate the Manchester United team of Law, Best and Charlton. The fans demanded a certain type of player, similar to the skilful player favoured at Spurs, and he felt that I fitted in with his scheme. He was also trying to sign Trevor Francis.

In the end I decided to stay at Spurs, although it was a difficult choice. Now, I know I made the right decision – Spurs went on to the win the FA Cup in successive seasons.

There have always been plenty of hints from foreign clubs, although you could never really tell how serious they were. The exception was Naples – they were so keen that in 1983 they paid for my family holiday in a little seaside town outside the city. We stayed at the El Cid Hotel, which was smashing – in fact I have recommended the place to a few friends. Unfortunately for Naples, that old Achilles' injury got in the way of another possible move, and the transfer broke down before it really got started.

My one regret when I left was never having won the Championship – the title has eluded me so far, and has also eluded Spurs since they won the double in 1961. The achievements of the double team had always been stuffed down my throat, especially in my early years at Spurs. Of course, it's lovely to be associated with a club with such great traditions, but it's pretty hard to live with sometimes, notably when the team is going through a lean spell. Also, no matter how well you play or how successful you become, the fans make comparisons with the double side, and you tend to come off second best. So far, the only compensation I can offer is that the last generation team won at Anfield, which even the great teams of Tottenham's past failed to do – and what is more, we won there twice.

Nothing worthwhile comes easy, nor should it – appreciation is so important in life. The fact that my move to Monaco wasn't made easily makes me value it even more. When the time came I had four solid offers to move from Tottenham. There was an approach from Celtic, but with David Hays' situation changing the prospects waned. In any case my heart was set on a move abroad. Paris St Germain were very interested and their representatives came to London to watch me play. They were impressed when I scored against Oxford, one of the best goals of my career. Atletico Madrid made a move, but everything was up-in-the-air at the club because of presidential elections and a change of manager. After waiting 12 years for a move to the Continent I couldn't risk holding on until they were ready, even though I might have been very tempted to move to Spain.

Monaco came into the contest very late in the day. In the end it became a straight choice between the two French clubs. My final season with Spurs was coming to a close. I was delighted that we had beaten Watford and that my last game for the club would be the FA Cup final at Wembley.

David Pleat had been negotiating with Paris St Germain, who were clearly the front runners for my signature. As far as the manager was concerned they were the club I would be going to. But Spurs and Paris St Germain could not come to a successful conclusion in their negotiations over the fee. The fact that these dragged on for so long gave Monaco the opportunity to make their late bid. I gathered Spurs were unhappy that an acceptable price could not be agreed, but I had concluded all my side of the bargaining. My wife Anne and myself had been to Paris, and everything was settled – except that is with Spurs. Chairman Irving Scholar had a meeting with the club, but the stalemate continued. Ironically, after Irving's frustrating talks with Paris St Germain he agreed a fee with Monaco in two minutes!

The Paris club were furious when I signed for Monaco. They publicly criticised me for 'breaking a promise'. The truth was, quite simply, that I had agreed to sign for Paris St Germain provided that they were able to reach a successful deal with Spurs. That they were clearly unable to do. I had not promised to play for Paris unconditionally – there was no question of going back on my word. I spent two days in Paris with Anne looking at houses and schools for Zoe. However, there was no doubt that the day I was finally due, after 12 long years, to join a Continental club turned into a French farce. One minute I was flying out to join Paris St Germain, and the next my destination changed to Monaco.

It was a Sunday, Anne, the children and I were at home in Harlow packing our bags, tickets at the ready. At three o'clock that afternoon we were off to Paris. But while my head said it had to be Paris, my heart still wanted to go to Monaco.

We had been to Monaco on a fact-finding mission and had fallen in love with the place. The club were very ambitious. They were buying five new players, determined to put Monaco back on the soccer map. There were so many positive vibrations. On the other hand, I had spoken to Ossie Ardiles about Paris St Germain. He had experienced a loan deal with them during the problems over the Falklands, and while he didn't say anything bad about them, he warned me to watch their promises very closely and to make sure everything was written into the contract. So there was a slight feeling of disappointment as Anne and I packed knowing it would have to be Paris. But we had made up our minds, and were both determined that we would make the most of the move.

Thirty minutes before we were due to walk out of the front door the 'phone rang. It was Dennis Roach, my agent. He had been in touch with Monaco, and the deal was on. When we left we would be flying to Monaco instead. I could hardly believe it. Ironically, a few hours before I had been watching on television a preview of the Monaco Grand Prix which was to start that Monday.

The first time I visited Monaco, the new coach, Arsène Wenger, had been away. Nevertheless, the whole atmosphere at the club had been so appealing – everything felt right somehow. That feeling was reinforced when I arrived and met the coach. He is a young man, full of ideas and enthusiasm. He told me the type of player he wanted and explained the set-up of the team. My mind was made up there and then. I stayed at the Beach Plaza, a beautiful hotel in Monte Carlo with a private beach that Princess Caroline sometimes uses in the summer. Who could fail to be captivated by such a magical part of the world?

Mark Hateley had of course signed for Monaco, and it was certainly an advantage to have Mark and his family there. But that was not the reason for my decision. I could see the sense in signing for Monaco for reasons outside football. It just felt right in Monaco, for me and my family. And as it has turned out I am happy playing my football there too.

I've heard a lot of criticism of my move – that I've come just for the money, for instance. It's utter nonsense. Let's get one thing straight. I might have preferred to have gone to Juventus or Barcelona, but I did not have an offer from either club. It might have appeared a more ambitious move had I gone to Italy or Spain, but there were no offers from Italy and the only approach from Spain was too confused to be relied upon. I had no option. It was French football or nothing.

In the end I chose to do what I felt was right in my heart. I'm a believer in God, as I've explained, and sometimes God tests you. He provided an answer half an hour before I was due to leave for Paris – what a test of faith for anybody! Once again, however, I have been savagely criticised for my decision. It seems, no matter what I do, or where I go, I'm bound to get stick from someone. Those who say I have come to Monaco just for the money are looking at my situation through their own eyes; if they were in my place they would see things differently. I never put money first in my life. Those who say I am motivated by money don't know me or appreciate my beliefs.

The people who criticise French football haven't a clue. Most of them have probably never seen it for themselves. The national side has reached two World Cup semi-finals and has won the Nations Cup. Michel Platini was very special, but the rest of that team played in the French First Division. True, at this moment the national team is on a down, but football goes in cycles. Of course my critics are entitled to air their opinions, but I don't regret my move to French football, no matter what people say. I have no doubt that the game here is better than in Italy. I'm equally sure that English football supporters would prefer the quick, exciting, robust French style to the slower Italian approach. I've learned a lot about Italian football from Mark Hateley. He was a hero in his first season, but after three years he was quite happy to get out.

I am enjoying every minute of my time here. I feel as though I've been in Monaco for six or seven years. I'm so glad it worked out that I came abroad at the age of 30 – I'm mature now and able to adapt. I have the benefit of a stable home background, and it's fortunate that a vital stage of my life had begun to blossom as I was about to leave England. I was only really half a person until, as I became aware of God, my life as a Christian evolved. Somebody told me that I was very brave to divulge my innermost thoughts in this book. On the contrary, it wasn't courageous – if something that important happens in someone's life, it would be cowardly not to discuss it. I might not have been able to live with myself had I not revealed my beliefs. In fact, I'm delighted by the way they were portrayed.

I was born English, and proud of it. But had I been born Italian or French, no one would have ever questioned my commitment to skill, invention and artistic football that pleases the fans and gives me so much pleasure. I'm suited to French, or indeed, Italian football. It's a delight to be playing in France, quite simply because they respect skill so much. The technical side of the game is paramount here. I'm not saying that the Tottenham supporters didn't appreciate me –

they didn't want me to leave. In fact, it may well be that the Spurs fans value me more now that I've gone. If that is the case, it's no surprise. It's like a marriage: it is based on love, but because you are living in each other's pockets for so long it can break up. Then when you are apart you miss each other. That's how it is with Spurs and myself.

Emphasis on skills is part of the French mentality and is shared by the majority of the Continental nations. Here in France they are more concerned with the offensive side of the game. The Monaco manager and the fans don't want to see me charging around making crunching tackles. There are other players in the team designated for that task. My function is purely creative. That is something I have always wanted. Now I have it. Why should that be so wrong?

It might not go down well with English fans, even those brought up on the skills of teams like Spurs and West Ham, where they try to build from the back. English supporters are frustrated far too quickly when they see the defenders inter-passing or the goalkeeper throwing the ball out rather than thumping it up the field. Italian football is all about getting everyone behind the ball as fast as possible to frustrate the opposition. It is very slow. That would not go down well with the English fans. French football is played at a level between the extremes of the Italian and English games.

Here in Monaco I'm content, rejuvenated. I have a better lifestyle, for myself and my family. I don't like comparing Monaco with Tottenham. I loved all those years I spent with Spurs, but I'm more enthusiastic about my football than I was in the last year or so at Tottenham. I urgently needed a change and I was beginning to think I would never fulfil my ambition to play on the Continent. Now life couldn't be better. Monte Carlo is the ideal place to bring up children. There is no crime at all, and it's so very clean.

Mark and I live in the same apartment block. The Hoddles are on the sixth floor, the Hateleys on the ninth. There may not be enough space in Monte Carlo for houses and gardens, but the apartment has everything we need. There are four bedrooms, and it's 20 yards from the beach. Some days it's a thrill just to pull back the curtains and gaze out at the Mediterranean and the clear, blue sky. We have a beautiful view and a large balcony from which to enjoy it. The principality is a lovely place, and the whole of the Côte D'Azur is within easy reach.

I was a little concerned at first about Zoe's schooling. She's at the age when she's starting school, and I suppose it would have been a difficult time even if we had been back in Harlow. Fortunately she settled in quickly at a lovely little school actually in the football stadium. It's part of the American school which is based in Nice.

Mark and I take the kids to school at 8.30am, and then go on to training at 9.30am. The training is longer and harder than we were used to in England, but the setting couldn't be matched anywhere in the world. Sometimes we train at the stadium, sometimes 1,500 feet up in the Monaco mountains. Even in the winter the temperatures can reach 70 degrees. On occasions it is a little chilly in the mountains, but normally we're training in the winter sunshine. The stadium has been built on reclaimed land. The football pitch is on the third level above car parking space, an Olympic-sized swimming pool, a basketball stadium, weight rooms, an apartment block for apprentices, business premises and a gym.

People live in apartments in Monte Carlo with lifts to the car parking space below ground. They can leave their homes by car and drive to the stadium car park, taking a lift to their seats, without ever getting wet, even if it is pouring outside. That must be unique in football. Prince Albert is a keen football follower. He goes to all the big Monaco games, and I've spotted him training with the players. He represented Monaco in the bobsleigh in the winter Olympics, an event for which he trained for a year. I was once introduced to him on a match day, but I didn't know who he was! He turned up in Dr Marten's and cut-down Levis, sporting a rucksack. We shook hands and I walked on past him – I was taken aback when someone told me who he was.

Monte Carlo is a tax-free haven, a playground for the rich and famous. There are plenty of tennis stars like Boris Becker and Bjorn Borg, racing drivers, mostly when the Grand Prix is in town, and film stars. I haven't learned the language too well, but there has hardly been the need. There is such a big American and English community that English is spoken almost more often than French. It may be a very rich place, but there are a lot of unhappy people walking around. Sometimes money can be the root of all evil, and it certainly doesn't guarantee happiness. I believe that to be unhappy is the worst thing in life.

As I said, money doesn't rule my life and that's why I will always insist I did not come here for that reason. I am furthering my career and my outlook on life. I've learned a lot as a person, as I suspected I would, by coming overseas and broadening my horizons. I was stale at Spurs – if I had stayed there I wouldn't be as bubbly as I feel now. That is not down to a champagne lifestyle but a result of the fresh challenge for my football. I can also spend more time with my family, and know that the children are growing up in an ideal environment. Of course I'm earning good money, I always have done in my career. I play football at a high level and if a club like Monaco offer me a great deal to play for them I would be an idiot to turn them down.

I'm a very private person. I do some things with my money that I would not want to publicise. I do a lot of work for charities, but that is a personal matter. Mark is out here earning as much money as I am. He's much younger, but he does not attract the same sort of criticism as I seem to.

I don't like to look too far into the future – I've never been one to tempt fate. Everything can come to an end tomorrow with one bad injury, and things have a nasty habit of changing in life. I signed a two-year contract with Monaco with a year's option. I'm happy at the moment to stay, to enjoy my football and my lifestyle, but I'm a realist.

At the halfway stage of the season Monaco enjoyed a three-point lead at the top of the First Division. Nothing would give me greater satisfaction than to win the first Championship medal of my career and then play in the European Cup for the first time. I've always believed that the only place to answer your critics is on the pitch.

There were many times in England when I felt as though I was hitting my head against a brick wall by the way I was playing the game. In any other country the team would have been built around me and I would have won 100 caps by now. Instead the old question about whether my style is suited to the national team cropped up again after I'd been playing in France for just a couple of months. England's first international of the new season was in West Germany against the host nation for the European Championships. England have developed a notorious habit of starting slowly in recent seasons. For some reason the results have been poor and our games that autumn prompted the use of the phrase 'Black September'. The match in Dusseldorf was no exception. We lost and didn't play well.

The whole team were bad on the day, but I was made the scapegoat. I was dropped for the next match against Turkey at Wembley in the European Championship qualifying tie. I'm convinced that the manager made his decision to leave me out immediately after the West Germany match. I couldn't see the justice in his decision. If ever I became a manager, and I had a player who had played well for me over a period of time, I would not be inclined to leave him out after just one bad game . . . especially when the whole side had performed badly.

There was much speculation in the Press before the Wembley game against Turkey about whether I would be left out. Bobby Robson made the trip to Monaco to watch me play, but my instincts told me that he had already made up his mind. The manager told me the day before the Turkey game that I had not been picked. I expected it, but it was not easy to take. For weeks I had endured criticisms of my decision to play in French football, but I said little or nothing publicly in response. What I felt and what I had to say, I said privately to the manager when we had a talk about the decision. I had more to say than he did.

I told him I felt that I had been left out unfairly and that I had been made the scapegoat for what went wrong in Germany. I could understand the manager looking to the future by his selection of young Neil Webb of Nottingham Forest. I didn't feel angry – I have to take decisions like that in my stride, there's no point in crying about them. I simply explained a few things to Bobby, such as the way I was playing in Monaco, the way I was expected to play. I told him I was playing there to benefit my game, my style, not for the motives people were suggesting. I explained that my job at my club was not about running back and tackling. My role was to express myself and let others concern themselves with man-to-man marking. We had two strong players in midfield for such a task. In fact, after two or three games, the coach told me not to go so far deep for the ball and to concentrate entirely on the attacking aspects of my play.

Bobby Robson assured me that I was still a big part of his plans for the European Championships, but players have been told that before. He said it was 'up to me', explaining that I had to be playing well for both Monaco and England. Naturally, I felt very disappointed and let down, but there was no animosity between myself and Bobby Robson. Of course, I felt frustrated, too. I had gone back a few years to the same old dilemma. The naturally gifted individual is the one to be disposed of first. It's that aspect of the England mentality that I dislike so much, but I'm English and have to put up with it.

I accept that the system in the England team is different. But I'm playing to instructions with Monaco, and there is no reason why I cannot adapt to the England way. Unfortunately, I've had to accept that the national side is built around players like Bryan Robson, while on the Continent the team is built around players like me. I took the decision on the chin, and I believe I handled it correctly. I told Bobby Robson that I was determined to get back into the side.

Luckily I had to wait only 45 minutes for my chance. I came on as a second-half substitute for the injured Trevor Steven, and although I played in a position that doesn't suit me, wide on the right, I proved that I still retain my enthusiasm for representing my country.

I was so glad that I was able to play again so soon and that it was for the entire second half. I also came on in the European Championship tie in Yugoslavia. But my problem was how to get back into the side. Certainly, missing the friendly in Isreal did not help. The timing of Monaco's 'pre-season' games after the winter mid-season break meant that England's match clashed with Monaco's friendly at Spurs. However much I wanted to play again at Spurs, the match in Tel Aviv would have been important to my chances of resurrecting my England career.

Then again, the question of club commitments has arisen with other England players, and it has not affected their international chances. The England manager knows I want to be available whenever I can. Regrettably for Mark and myself, the Monaco fixture made it impossible for us to be available at that time, and Bobby Robson understood and respected this.

The match at White Hart Lane was part of the transfer package between Monaco and Spurs. My transfer fee was £800,000 and, added to the gate receipts from the friendly, the final sum Spurs were paid for me was £1 million. That was good business. Chairman Irving Scholar kept his word that he would let me go a year before my contract expired, but at the same time he did the best possible deal for his club. The parting of the ways from Tottenham after so many years at the club was not as difficult as I had anticipated. However, it was very disappointing to lose to Coventry in the FA Cup final. When I walked off the pitch at Wembley, knowing it had been my final game for Spurs, I felt emotional. I regretted the dismay of the club and the fans more than the defeat itself.

I knew all along that the physical act of leaving Spurs

would be OK because I had been resigned to going for such a long time. I knew the next stage of my life was just beginning. I had no regrets then, and I have none now. Spurs were the club I loved as a kid, when I supported them from the terraces, and my feelings for them will never change. However, I was staggered by the hurtful remarks made by David Pleat once I had signed for Monaco. He said he was surprised that I had passed the medical, that without me Spurs would be a better, more efficient, team with a greater chance of winning the Championship. I just had to laugh at it all. I couldn't understand why he did it. It seemed strange to me that he had to resort to such cheap jibes at departing players. I was not alone in being on the receiving end of such treatment – he had had some stinging farewell words for Graham Roberts, as I related earlier, and Richard Gough, too. It seemed that, for whatever reason, he could not resist it.

Yet Pleat began his first season as Spurs manager by giving me a totally free role, wanting me to be his Platini. That soon went out of the window: he dropped me for the Norwich game; he reinstated me after I played well for England against Yugoslavia; finally he changed the entire Spurs system to build the midfield around me by playing five there. That formation worked a treat. The confidence within the team soared and we went on to reach the FA Cup final.

When I look back on David Pleat as Tottenham manager I simply can't work him out. He had sound football ideas, but he complicated things by trying to be too clever. He sometimes left players out when he shouldn't have done and messed around with the system when it didn't need it. Afterwards he regretted it, and he did learn from his mistakes.

Off the field, he transformed the club. Spurs are a big club, but under Keith Burkinshaw and Peter Shreeve they had nonetheless become a homely and friendly one. Watford and Wimbledon built their reputations on such a principle, and it even helped them to achieve success. I'm not saying a club the size of Spurs should be like Watford or Wimbledon, but no matter how big, the players should be able to relax and enjoy themselves as well as tackle their roles in a professional way. Until Pleat arrived at the club the players were able to mix happily with the directors. Discipline was not affected, and the players certainly had no less respect for the directors, as some people suggested. Once Pleat arrived none of the players were permitted to go into the directors' room, and access to other areas of the club was denied to them. The whole atmosphere at White Hart Lane changed drastically. Maybe that sort of regime had worked for Pleat at Luton and he wanted a similar system at Spurs, but in my view it created negative waves.

Don't get me wrong. I am not for one minute suggesting he was a bad manager for us. On the contrary, I thought he had many bright ideas and he had a good, very dry sense of humour. In fact, he was a very funny man, and a good manager. What happened to him at Spurs, and the circumstances of his departure, left me feeling very sorry for him. I don't know all the facts, so it would not be right for me to pass judgement on Pleat or anyone else. Whatever the rights and wrongs, no one should suffer the way he did. In that kind of situation football takes a back seat, but from a distance it did look as though the club had no choice but to let him go.

It is sad that in the first season since I left the club they have experienced such turmoil. There was clearly a very difficult time between Pleat's departure and the arrival of Terry Venables. I'm delighted that Spurs have chosen Terry for the job. If you are a top jockey who wants to win the Derby and you are given the choice of the top three horses you would pick the one you think has the best chance of winning the race. Spurs believe they have picked the best manager to win them the Championship, and I would back their judgement. Of course, there's no guarantee that Spurs will be successful, but they have given themselves the best possible chance.

In the 1988-89 season he will be determined to prove he is the tops, particularly as he will want to demonstrate his suitability to become England manager one day. Terry

Venables cannot be judged at the moment – the team he inherited is not his team. The time to make a judgement will be during his first full season at White Hart Lane.

I have made no secret of my admiration for Terry Venables from the moment I worked with him at England Under-21 level. I loved his vision, his ideas about attacking football. So many coaches know how to be defensive, how to stop others playing, and that's what has been wrong with the game in England for so many years. Certainly defensive football is part of the game, and Terry knows as much as anyone about how to stop the opposition from playing, but that side of the game isn't too difficult. I could find you dozens of Sunday morning team coaches who could manage that.

We have got to the stage in English football where even the centre-forward is given a coaching manual about how to defend from the front. A team needs a blend of attack and defence, and Terry is the man to come up with the right mix. Although I admire him for his attacking philosophies, Terry also has his own stern defensive tactics. Spurs fans may have to get used to the idea of a strong back four with offside tactics, but I'm sure they will adjust to that if it produces exciting football and good results. In fact, the most successful Spurs side since the double team adopted the offside trap with great effect. The back four of Steve Perryman, Graham Roberts, Paul Miller and Chris Hughton had those tactics off to a tee. It wasn't pretty to watch, especially away from home, but it proved to be highly successful.

I would love to have played for Terry at Spurs – he would have been so good for me. In a way, I envy some of the good, young players coming through the ranks at the club who will flourish under Terry's expert tuition. I'm sure it would have benefited my career had I played for him there when I was a teenager. I am very pleased that my old club have acquired such a gifted coach and manager, and I wish him every success in the future.